PRAISE FOR

"Doctor Travis Hearne is a gifted thought leader who brings his unique mix of energy, enthusiasm, creativity and intellect to every challenge, every day. Having served with Travis in uniform, I have had the great fortune to work closely with this inspirational professional in one of the most demanding, dynamic, and fast-paced operating environments in the US military. He is one of our very finest, a selfless and accomplished leader, coach, and visionary."

—Lieutenant General (Ret) Charles D. Luckey,
United States Army, 33rd Chief,
United States Army Reserve

"If you are the leader of hybrid staff, regardless of where you are in the process—the beginning, the middle, or the end of your rope—Hybrid is the book you need to read! It refreshes tried and true management principles and applies them to the new world of on-site/off-site work with engaging stories and anecdotes. There are practical solutions to the unique challenges of today's workplace and workforce that you will be able to immediately implement. I particularly appreciated the realistic scenarios supported by solid academic research. Hybrid is a terrific readable resource for those of us wrestling with the complexities of leading others every day."

—Gregory Gast, SPHR, Chief Human
Resources Officer, Sun River Health

"Travis Hearne has written the future of hybrid team leadership. He confronts the wicked problems facing us today—not just managing but leading teams in increasingly complex work environments. Hybrid captures your attention through rich storytelling, thought-provoking critiques of traditional approaches to teaming, and clear insights for leading in our new normal."

—*Dr. Jennifer L. Phillips, Assistant Professor in the Doctoral program of Organizational Change and Leadership, USC Rossier School of Education*

"Hybrid is a must-have book for anyone who leads others, for it is rich in research and suggestions on how to lead and manage remote or hybrid employees. If you believe you can lead others in hybrid settings the same way you have in the past, you are sorely mistaken. Dr. Hearne is a seasoned leader, solidified by his time in the military and now in the corporate world. He speaks from personal experience as well from an academic standpoint bring and brings them both into the 'new' office structure of our day. If you believe you can lead others in hybrid settings the same way you have in the past, you are sorely mistaken. Dr. Hearne, shows us how to lead these teams, and lead them well."

—*Dr. Brent D. Garrison, Author of Leadership by the Book, President of By the Book Consulting*

"During a time where remote leadership has become the new norm, there has also become inherent challenges in true transformational leadership within this remote culture. So, who do we turn to for guidance and support with this adjustment? Dr. Travis Hearne has come to save us and sets the guidelines of creating a culture in which people feel individually considered, inspired, and motivated through empathy and support but doing so in a non-face-to-face culture, remotely."

*—Dr. **Lucas Dyer**, Sr. Program Manager*
Learning and Development, Amazon

"Hybrid does a great job of connecting proven leadership techniques with emerging workplace needs. The global pandemic forced all leaders to revisit assumptions about remote productivity. Successful organizations will need to adopt a long-term mindset towards hybrid work approaches. Every modern leader needs to add the skills shared in Hybrid to their leadership toolkit."

*—Dr. **Candace Givens**,*
Executive Leader, People Champion

"Health, natural disasters, war, global markets, international business teams, changing lifestyles, and constant changes in our world's economy demand that organizational leadership change in order to survive. Dr. Hearne offers an organizational compass for leaders to navigate these chaotic times as hybrid organizational leadership continues to demonstrate a solution for today's world. Dr. Hearne's clear, concise, and personable writing style will benefit the seasoned leader as well as the person working into new leadership opportunities. This book is an enjoyable and uplifting read that will benefit any organization finding themselves in the midst of transitioning and improving a hybrid model of hybrid organizational leadership."

—*Dr. Theodore J. Wiard, Director of Trauma, Grief and Renewal Program at Southwestern College*

HYBRID

DR. TRAVIS MICHAEL HEARNE

HYBRID

A GUIDE FOR SUCCESSFULLY
LEADING ON-SITE AND
REMOTE TEAMS

ILLUMIFY
MEDIA.COM

Published by
Illumify Media Global
www.IllumifyMedia.com
"Let's bring your book to life!"

Library of Congress Control Number: 2022912192

Paperback ISBN: 978-1-955043-82-3

Typeset by Art Innovations (http://artinnovations.in/)
Cover design by Debbie Lewis

Printed in the United States of America

To all of the amazing leaders out there, struggling to adapt in this new world of leadership: we are all in this together, and we will not only get through this, but we will thrive in this new world. Thank you for working so hard for your people.

This book is also dedicated to my late mother who passed away during this journey. Mom, you were my biggest cheerleader, and I know that you are looking down on us and smiling.

CONTENTS

INTRODUCTION

Welcome to a new and exciting work world where we are unbound by location, time, or operating hours! We live in exciting professional times where hybrid work environments are becoming more and more common. Employees and leaders now have a daily choice in where they want to work. Thoughts of the morning commute are now replaced by, "Should I roll out of bed, throw on a collared shirt, and log on? Maybe I'll hit the gym and take my meeting on the treadmill. How about I head to that new and trendy coffee shop with the free wifi downtown. Or should I hop into the office and see who's there?"

Amazing, right?! In the past, for many of us, the idea of working from home was so beyond the realm of possibility that we never gave it a second thought. But were we ready for a global pandemic to force us out of the building? While it all seems so great at times, let's look at the other side of the coin through the lens of leadership. Many of us leaders really didn't have a choice in the matter. So how do we lead well in this new environment?

Leadership can be defined as the *action* of leading a group of people or an organization. The key word there is action. How in the world are we supposed to lead hybrid and virtual teams in an action-packed way? How do we continue to scale our businesses, connect with and motivate our people, create new products, and generate innovative ideas *all* over a computer screen and often times across the country? *Hybrid* will guide you through some of the best practices to do just that.

Hybrid is a fully loaded vehicle that drives you through a new leadership environment, where leaders must learn how to lead and manage their people, institute and facilitate organizational change, and generate successful outcomes for their businesses while managing on-site and remote employees. By looking at tried and true leadership and organizational change models and theory, *Hybrid* guides leaders through a new way of thinking and leading. Leadership gurus such as Dr. James Burns, Dr. Urie Bronfenbrenner, and Dr. John Kotter have already provided us with frameworks for which to work and thrive in hybrid and remote work environments. These aren't *new* concepts; we are just applying them to a *new* working environment where our workforces are sent out of the boardroom and into the living room.

We have to learn how to lead and manage these teams toward success using the tools already at our disposal. But we can't use a screwdriver to hammer in the nails. We, as leaders, must take a look at the toolbox, figure out which ones we need, and adjust the plan as necessary—*Hybrid* will show you how to do that.

Leadership and management are two wildly distinct, yet tightly intertwined, concepts. Both are difficult to do well, even under the most pristine and straightforward circumstances. Throw in a new policy that forces you and your entire staff out of cubicle farms and corner offices and into basements and kitchens, and the difficulty multiplies dramatically. It's like throwing water on an already wonky machine and expecting it not only to work correctly but to perform even better than before.

As businesses and organizations morph into a new and exciting model of their previous selves, leaders must learn how to adapt and flourish in this new working environment. Businesses, small and large, must create a new way to thrive, scale, lead, manage, and change with a new hybrid workforce. While all of this is challenging, *Hybrid* brings us good news here.

One thing we have going for us is that hybrid and remote work models are hardly new concepts. In 2001, the *Wall Street Journal* reported that more than half of companies with over five thousand employees used virtual teams with leaders spread out across different areas of the country.[1] T Since the early 2000's, researchers have predicted that the virtual work environment trend would increase as it became more technologically efficient and more financially beneficial.[2] What was not accounted for was a global pandemic that would force businesses, government institutions, and otherwise "business in-person" organizations to embrace a new virtual leadership reality.

As of September 2021, corporate giants like Apple, Cisco, Ford, Microsoft, and Target have moved to a permanent hybrid workforce that gives employees the option of how and where they want to work. The world of corporate leadership and management has changed forever. Leaders must be equipped with the correct tools to change progressively with the times and lead and manage hybrid and remote teams.

Here's a brief story of how I walked through this exact situation. It may sound familiar. I experienced the inadequacy of being a leader thrown into hybrid leadership and felt the pain firsthand of being disconnected and disoriented.

Carl Sagan stated, "You have to know the past to understand the present." Okay, let's go back to November of 2019. A simpler time. The United States presidential impeachment trial was the sole focus of media outlets across the globe. Our televisions were inundated with debates, and waves of civil unrest following numerous and unimaginable tragedies actively dividing our country further.

Behind the scenes, it seemed, a war in Afghanistan waged with no realistic end in sight, surpassing its twentieth anniversary. While these tragic realities cut and nipped at the American fabric, most Americans did what they do best: they persevered. Unemployment hit a record low, and we celebrated the American women's soccer World Cup victory. NASA successfully conducted the first-ever, all-woman spacewalk, and the Washington Nationals defeated the Houston Astros, winning their inaugural World Series title.

The world was still spinning. There were no mask or vaccine mandates, restaurants were packed, schools were open, concerts were kickin', and it was a golden era of easy, carefree travel around the world. Where I live, we Coloradoans were ecstatic about what the *Farmer's Almanac* called a "polar coastal winter," meaning there would be feet of fresh, skiable powder falling throughout Summit County very soon.

The news cycle continued to buzz with an almost white-noise kind of consistency, when all of a sudden, things began to shift. In December, 2019 the white noise changed from impeachment and civil unrest to coverage of the first case of a rare and highly contagious virus in Wuhan, China. Like many of you, I initially watched this unfold with tangential apprehension at best. I felt deep concern for the people of China, but I was sure that this was going to be a controlled incident as we had seen with previous outbreaks. There's no way it was going to make it all the way across the globe. Or so we thought . . .

In March of 2020, the World Health Organization declared COVID-19 a global pandemic, shutting down borders across the globe and causing most global industries and businesses to grind to a dramatic and immediate halt. The S&P 500 took a 30 percent plunge and by May, the U.S. unemployment rate hit 14.7 percent, the worst rate since the Great Depression, with 20.5 million people out of work—a dumbfounding shift from only a few short months ago.[3] Four weeks turned into eight, and eight turned into twelve, and it became our national priority to "flatten the curve."

The global economy was changed forever. At the time, I was working as the Chief Interagency and Operations Officer for an element of the Department of Defense responsible for defending the homeland. Our job was to ensure that the United States, Canada, and Mexico were protected from any number of threats and vulnerabilities, a gargantuan task. For the past year and a half leading up to the pandemic, our mighty fifteen-person rock star of a team was as tight as one could get. The flow in which we worked was impressive.

Our people had an outstanding work-life balance, and they seemed to be very happy with their jobs. And then on the morning of March 13, 2020, my inbox began to overflow with messages from the commander's office. The first batch of emails ordered us to go down to 50 percent manning which meant that our team could only spend 4 hours a day in the building. I thought, *Okay, we can still do that. We can cut down their daily*

hours using some fancy human resources tools and make that work.
We were going to cut the team in half and split up a twelve-
hour workday. Easy peasy! By the afternoon of that same day, we
got the notice from our four-star commanding general that our
three-person leadership team was the only team allowed in our
offices (a space built for fifteen), and the rest of our team would
have to begin working remotely immediately.

We had to split a twenty-four-hour day into three separate
shifts, only overlapping them by thirty minutes. How on earth
were we supposed to do our jobs? We were the Department of
Defense—being able to do our work effectively was *literally* a
matter of national security. How in the world would I make
sure the homeland defense boulder was continuously pushed
uphill while we completely changed the environment in which
we worked?

So, as any good Marine would do, I leaned on my previous
training and created a plan—a plan so great that it would fail
four times before it actually worked. I started with three-times-
a-day virtual meeting rotation. Fail. Okay, how about once a
week? Fail. Fine, we will meet on Monday and Friday. Fail. After
banging my head against the wall for about two weeks, I realized
that I needed some help. I had never had to figure out a problem
quite like—I had to turn to the experts on this one. I looked at
myself in the mirror and said, *Okay, all of those failures have to be
some sort of playbook for success, right?*

I started digging into every leadership and organizational
change book I had collected over the years, and looked for
help. I needed to look at this problem through the eyes of Dr.
Urie Bronfenbrenner, Dr. James Burns, and Dr. James Kotter. I
poured over Dr. John C. Maxwell's literature on leadership and

change. There just had to be something in all of this foundational leadership and change theory that could be used to answer the organizational calculus problem I had been handed.

The good news was that there was more material on organizational change and leadership than I could ever fully understand. The bad news was that there was more material on organizational change and leadership than I could ever fully understand. Again, leaning on my Marine Corps metaphors I was so proud of, I began to size up this massive hill I was about to take. But now I had the ammunition I needed to get the job done. Theory in hand, I began to ask questions of my staff, listen to their concerns, and watch as this calculus problem turned into basic math. My focus had to be on my people and what they needed during this intensely stressful period of history, and how we could best work together toward mission accomplishment.

So that's how we got here, with you walking with me in this crazy leadership journey that will undoubtedly change, get better, and then worse, and then better again. After each chapter I've included some "Questions to Consider" and "Transformational Tips" to help you put these lessons to work for you and your specific challenges. Use these as a guide to analyze challenges, create solutions, and lead your teams well. Leading is hard! I'm glad you are here, trusting me to walk you through some of my failures and successes. Together we can take care of our people and scale in business at the same time. Let's learn how.

ONE

TRANSFORMATIONAL LEADERSHIP
Inspiring and Motivating Individuals

H ank is the CEO of an up-and-coming technology company with over forty thousand employees, and they are thriving! He is in his mid-sixties, loves to wear dapper five-thousand-dollar suits, and bask in the glorious hierarchy he has created from the ground up. Having worked hard his entire life, Hank has reached the peak of the leadership mountain. As CEO, he sits in his corner office and barks orders at his administrative assistant, Traci, who rigorously types and takes notes on any orders he gives.

Traci is his brain, his calendar, his scribe, his proverbial punching bag, and his property—or at least that's the way she feels. She graduated summa cum laude with her undergraduate degree in computer science and engineering but works sixty-five hours a week fetching coffee, lunch, dry cleaning, and setting up meetings because every email or phone call her boss receives must go through her before it reaches his precious and more valuable inbox. Working without compliments, raises, or a hint of care for who she is as a person, she gets up every morning and wonders, *Will this be the day that I wake up and leave this crazy place?* Worse off, she isn't alone in this transactional and prison-like work environment. He treats everyone this way.

As the day winds down at around eighty thirty p.m., Traci finally goes home to an empty house, logs in to her university portal, and scrolls through the lengthy list of assignments she has due by morning. As her work cell continues to ring and beep at her, she silences it, opens a blank Word document, and begins the six-hour-a-night journey of becoming an MBA. And . . . scene. What . . . a . . . day . . .

This scenario may seem a bit dramatic and overly cinematic, but I promise you that this is, or was, the reality for so many people. Traci's boss, perched next to his automatic standing desk and carafe of high-dollar whiskey, is missing a huge opportunity to motivate Traci and even learn from her.

As extreme as this representation may seem, it strikes a few visceral and far too familiar chords within many of us. How often, as leaders, do we get so wrapped up in the tasks of the day or in our focus on successfully climbing the corporate ladder that we forget about the greatest asset we have—our people? We exchange personal connections and building trust for short-term results and half-baked ideas. When we do this, we miss out on the opportunity not only to impact someone's life but also to create long-lasting and impactful organizational change.

Let's change the story by fast-forwarding into the future and transforming it to fit our issue at hand. Two years later, Traci has broken free of her corporate prison, having earned her MBA, and is rising through the ranks of a *new* tech company with just a little over five thousand employees and a multimillion-dollar budget. Those late-night assignments and morning coffee runs are really paying off. Traci leads a diverse team of industry experts on the expansion of some of the most cutting-edge technological advancements on the planet. She leads her team with fairness, efficacy, efficiency, and devotion. Her ten-person team is a well-oiled machine, but at the same time, it can be challenging to manage and lead them since, as management and leadership are inherently hard, she is managing ten separate and dramatically different personalities.

Challenges that come with leadership are not lost on Traci. She works through the issues well and her team is happy. Ideas flow rapidly across the boardroom table and it's her job to translate them into a cohesive go-to-market strategy. Technological advancements are happening every day, and in this industry, if you aren't transforming, you're dying! She is thriving, being noticed, and, above all, transforming each of her team members into leaders.

Life is good—and then it happens. Traci is called into her boss's office and asked to sit in a chair that had been moved as close to the wall as it could possibly be. Traci's boss's face is as white as the marker board hung on his wall. She can tell he has no idea where to start, so he just spits it out. "The board has made the decision to move to a completely hybrid work model, and we have to figure out how to do that. Turns out, after comparing the benefits of remote and hybrid work, the C-suite has realized that by closing down offices across the country and sending most people home, we will save a ton of money by not having to rent office space. We plan to keep a few offices open in major cities from which people have the option of working, but the times of daily in-person boardroom meetings and random face-to-face interactions are now, seemingly, over."

The whole company is moving into a hybrid work model, where employees must work from home at least 80 percent of the time. Her team will have to rotate in and out of the office on different days of the week with as little overlap as possible, and she will have to learn to lead from a computer screen and a cell phone. Traci leaves her boss's office dumbfounded and a bit lost. Never in a million years did she think she would be in this position.

She thinks to herself, *It might be better to be back in my old job, with no leadership responsibilities at all. They didn't teach me anything about remote leadership in college.* As Traci gathers her thoughts and corrals her team together in the boardroom, she can already see the panic in their faces. The watercooler rumor mill has already begun to spin—her team knows what is coming. They have already heard about the change, and the panic has begun to set in.

Is the company going to survive? How am I going to feed my kids? What's going to happen to my salary? This is great; when can I start working from home?

These are the questions written on everyone's face that have not yet been verbalized. Before Traci can open her mouth, the room bursts with voices. Everyone has different concerns—personal, occupational, health, safety. She quickly realizes that this conversation is going nowhere and that the best way to do this is one-on-one. So, she clears the room and heads into her office to prepare for her biggest leadership test to date.

As she brings each of her team members into her office individually to discuss a way forward, a trend quickly emerges.

The majority of her staff wants to work strictly from home, without stepping foot into the office. Not only that, but they are ecstatic to start working from home. Two of her employees want to be in the office as much as possible because face-to-face interaction is important to them. All of them are flexible but have strong opinions on how and where they want to work. How is Traci going to create a work environment that is favorable to everyone's needs and wants and at the same time continue to succeed and thrive in the ever changing and always challenging industry of technology?

This leadership story epitomizes the organizational struggles that so many leaders have had to face since the beginning of the COVID-19 pandemic. In this scenario, Traci is going to have to figure out how to lead this hybrid team, and fast, so let's dive right into how transformational leadership theory can be extremely valuable in these types of situations by dissecting it into four key tenets: individual consideration, intellectual stimulation, inspirational motivation, and idealized influence.[1]

As much as you can actually define a theory, transformational leadership theory is characterized by Langston University as "a leadership approach that causes a change in individuals and social systems. In its ideal form, transformational leadership theory creates valuable and positive change in followers with the end goal of developing followers into leaders."[2]

It is true - culture eats strategy for breakfast! It is your job as the leader of a hybrid team to create a culture that is grounded in trust. Transformational leadership is a foundational tool that can be used to create a culture of trust and productivity. It's your job as the leader of this hybrid team to make sure the culture is as trusting and consistent as possible.

As we dissect transformational leadership a bit more, getting into the blood type and bone marrow of theoretical biology, we find that the foundational principles rely on a leader's ability to foster an environment and create a culture in which their people feel individually considered, inspired, and motivated. The leader promotes and demonstrates idealized influence and intellectually stimulates followers and the entire organization. The underlying core behind transformational leadership is that, when built on this framework, it can cement long-lasting and positive change within your people, increase their ability to lead, and change an entire organization for the better.

To understand the bones underneath the structural epidermis of transformational leadership, we must understand the man who corralled these concepts into theory. Dr. James MacGregor Burns codified the idea of transformational leadership in 1978 as the culmination of decades of research on political leadership. Dr. Burns was a Pulitzer Prize–winning presidential biographer and a pioneer in the study of leadership. He received his doctorate in government studies from Harvard University in 1947, later joining the Williams College faculty, where he taught until 1986. Dr. Burns, whom many consider the grandfather of transformational leadership theory, led the teaching of this concept for forty years across the globe. Dr. Burns published dozens of books and empirically challenged articles on leadership from 1947 until he died in 2014.

Before we dive into transformational leadership and the immense value it brings to hybrid and remote work environments, let's briefly get to know James MacGregor Burns. Before his Pulitzer was awarded and his academic and personal journey took flight, this man was a powerhouse! A literary mastermind with the ability to tell incredible stories about complex leadership situations. Knowing where Dr. Burns' leadership journey began gives us a clearer picture of why he was so emphatic about transforming leadership structures.

James Burns was born in Melrose, Massachusetts, in 1918 and was raised by his single mother. After completing his first round of academics at Williams College in 1937, he was drafted into the U.S. Army as a combat historian to serve in the Pacific during World War II. While enlisted in the army, he studied the history of United States politics and military organizations and the different structures by which they were led. Here, it seems, is where the spark for transformational leadership began.

According to the writings of Burns, whenever the term *leadership* or *leader* was mentioned, only military officers were ever involved in the conversation. At the time, and even today, military officers were thought to be more educated and experienced than those who enlisted. Burns saw this as a problem and verbalized his frustration with this concept early on in his military career. He would go on to write in his 1978 book entitled *Leadership*, "In real life, the most practical advice for leaders is not to treat pawns like pawns, nor princes like princes, but all persons like persons"; he also argues, "Power wielders may treat people as things. Leaders may not."[3] If we bring these quotes into the context of his military service, we begin to see transformational concepts emerge.

The hierarchical constructs by which our political and military systems were led were not producing the best potential outcome for our country. Furthermore, leaders with incredible potential were being overlooked by the simple fact that their title read "Enlisted." Dr. Burns's time spent in the army and on Capitol Hill began to shape his research. And thank goodness for that!

The focus of Dr. Burns's research revolved around the concept of transformational versus transactional leadership. He spent decades peeling back the onion of political and organizational leadership and how transactional it had all become. Dr. Burns found that transactional leadership, while necessary within certain constructs such as military organizations, was not conducive to long-term organizational or individual growth or success. Transactional leaders are hyper-focused on managing and supervising their employees rather than leading and challenging them. They are more interested in facilitating group performance through a performance-based leadership model rather than the personal growth of their people.

On the other hand, transformational leaders encourage their people to challenge the status quo and act as mentors. Motivation and inspiration are two of the most essential tools used by transformational leaders and equip them to pull followers outside their boxes and inspire innovative new ways of operating. The transformational leader knows who their people are and how each individual needs to be motivated. These leaders use this knowledge to create a culture of inclusion while instilling an infectious sense of pride in organizational accomplishment.

Individual Consideration

We'll kick things off by talking about individual consideration. The tenets of transformational leadership are not meant to be a sequential list of boxes to check. Still, each one of them intersects with the other in many different ways and can be used to different degrees based on the leadership challenge presenting itself. Individual consideration is very well defined by the phrase itself. It's the act of a leader listening and genuinely caring about what their people contribute.

It's a simple concept, but as we dive deeper into the context of individual consideration and its applicability in transformational leadership, the definition becomes richer and has a deeper meaning. Individual consideration refers to the degree to which the leader attends to each individual follower's needs, serves as a mentor or coach, and listens to the concerns and needs of their people. Giving empathy and support, the leader keeps communication open, and places challenges before the followers. Diving deeper, individual consideration is about respecting and celebrating followers' input and contributions toward actualizing the organizational vision and fulfilling the mission. Considering and acknowledging the personal accomplishments of your people will foster an environment where intrinsic motivation, based on internal drive, is commonplace, in place of extrinsic motivation, which is based on transactional outcomes of success.

As we venture a bit further, into the notion of hybrid work environments, I pose this question: does physical location make a difference in how you show individual consideration? Yes, there is something to physically sitting with someone to plan, innovate, reflect, and connect, but does this mean that being physically in the same room is the only way to individually consider our people?

The *Harvard Business Review* published "A Guide to Managing Your (Newly) Remote Workers." This article was published at the beginning of the shift to remote management due to COVID-19, and the first thing the authors talk about is concerns about the lack of face-to-face interaction in a hybrid or remote environment.[4]

Leaders and followers alike share their concern for not being able to interact in person. Leaders want to ensure accountability is maintained and to guide their people, and employees want to connect with their leader for guidance and direction. Psychologically speaking, social connection is good for our health.

Social connection is a pillar of lifestyle medicine. Humans are wired to connect, and this connection affects our health. From psychological theories to recent research, there is significant evidence that social support and feeling connected can help people maintain a healthy body mass index, control blood sugars, improve cancer survival, decrease cardiovascular mortality, decrease depressive symptoms, mitigate posttraumatic stress disorder symptoms, and improve overall mental health. The opposite of connection, social isolation, has a negative effect on health and can increase depressive symptoms as well as mortality.[5]

There really is something to human connection. Social and physical science is clear, and I'm not going to even hint at a proposition that social connection is unimportant. I am personally a strong proponent of physical and personal connection. I am *not* challenging the fact that social interaction is essential. However, I want to challenge the notion that this professional connection can only be accomplished in person. I want to push the professional boundary a bit here.

Research is beginning to show that employees are finding hybrid and remote environments to be more conducive to their individual work preferences. Surveys from the *Harvard Business Review* and the *New York Times* highlight several benefits people enjoy from hybrid and remote working environments. Things as simple as the nonexistent or significantly decreased commute time and the ability to throw a load of laundry in between meetings have extended employees' ability to be productive. Another item high on the list of perks is the ability to set up a personal workspace rather than working in a cubicle farm or corporate office. While these are perks of working from home or only coming into the office occasionally, these perks also open the door for leaders to show their people the individual consideration they need to succeed.

As a leader, you now have the ability to listen and to actualize your employees' respective ideal work environments, taking into consideration how each employee works best. Before the hybrid movement (I'm calling it that), employees found themselves slaves to a monotonous routine. Wake up in the morning, jump in the car, turn on your favorite morning show, and start your forty-five-minute commute to the office. Come into the office for at least eight and a half hours a day, take your thirty-minute lunch break (frequently at your desk), and then hop back in your car for another forty-five-minute commute back home. Wash, rinse, repeat. Hybrid and remote employees can smash the old molds of the preconceived workday by personalizing their space, time, and priorities (with guidance from you as the leader, of course).

As a transformational leader forced to lead your people from a distance, this is an amazing and simple opportunity to show individual consideration. As your people begin their hybrid and remote journeys, actively listen to their wants and needs for their workspaces and schedules. If appropriate and sustainable, allow flexibility in schedules and meeting times based on the availability of your people.

At this point in our journey with hybrid and remote environments, the technology is already in place to arrange meetings, sync schedules, and interact effectively. This is an opportunity for you as an outstanding transformational leader to take advantage of these technological advancements and create individual and team schedules that are conducive to organizational success while at the same time building up leaders who trust that you have their best interest in mind, all backed by consistent and persistent communication.

Communication is going to be a theme throughout this entire book, not just here. If this is new to you, I encourage you to acknowledge to your employees that there will be bumps in the road and that you will be there for them the entire way. Let them know that it's okay if Fluffy the cat suddenly jumps on your keyboard during a meeting, muting your microphone and spilling your water. Tell them to make arrangements so that this isn't a normal occurrence, but give them the grace they need to feel comfortable working from home.

Communicate a hybrid work schedule that works for them, you, and the team, but make it consistent. Schedules and routines, while recently disrupted, are human needs and can bring order to a chaotic environment. If they choose to come into the office for individual meetings with you on Mondays and as a team on Fridays, then set that schedule and keep it. This gives your staff input on their structure, but it will also help you maintain order and structure in your schedule.

As you look at each of your employees' physical spaces through the view of your computer monitor, comment on how they have set up their workspace. Compliment them on their choices and make suggestions. Do they have everything they need to be successful working remotely? Ask questions about their lives, goals, initiatives, thoughts, and dreams for their future. Craft individual development plans for each of your people based on the answers to these questions.

This all seems like a new employee orientation, but you can do this at any point. In fact, I recommend that this be a regularly occurring conversation—don't inundate them with questions about their life during every meeting, but check in regularly and intentionally. Help them follow through with their goals and what they want to accomplish over the next six months to a year or even more.

Intellectual Stimulation

Intellectual stimulation is a bit of a math problem when leading teams of more than four people. Going back to and building on individual consideration, leaders must understand what intellectually stimulates their people. Larger teams are going to have more diversity in what intellectual stimulation looks like. One employee may want to go back to school, while another just wants three hours a week to study and solve a work-related project of their own. This is where the communication piece continues to play a vital role.

Intellectual stimulation is the degree to which the leader challenges expectations, takes risks, asks for, and incorporates followers' ideas. An intellectual stimulator—that's the leader—encourages creativity and innovation, creating space for followers' ideas to flourish or even fail. This tenet is all about nurturing and developing your people as individual thinkers and creators. Let's look at a great example of using intellectual stimulation to transform an organization and an entire industry.

Dr. Edwin Catmull, the cofounder of Pixar and former President of Walt Disney Studios, started his career at his alma mater, the University of Utah, in their computer science department. Catmull was on the ground floor of groundbreaking experimental research in computer graphics in the late 1960s. At the time, the term *computer graphics* was as oxymoronic as jumbo shrimp or negative income. Dr. Catmull's research at the U of U was funded by the Advanced Research Projects Agency (ARPA), the organization which would eventually create what we now know as the internet.[6]

His work with the U of U and ARPA was meant to develop a way to animate, not with a pencil but with a computer. ARPA's mandate in all of this was to "support smart people in a variety of areas" and was predicated on the belief that researchers would try to do the right thing and overmanaging them was counterproductive. Dr. Catmull carried this mandate throughout his career, eventually expanding it during his creation of Pixar, sparking a cinematic revolution, one that no one thought would be possible. Dr. Catmull was given the freedom—and intellectual stimulation—to fulfill his computer animation goal, and television has never been the same.

This may seem like an uncommon example, but how do we know what our people are capable of without asking and giving them the opportunity to explore what that may be? Intellectual stimulation goes beyond giving employees challenging work.

It is about digging into the core of what stimulates them intellectually, personally, and professionally.

The hybrid or remote work environment is amazingly favorable to intellectual stimulation. For the most part, your people are already in the most comfortable environment possible to explore new things—their homes. Depending on the industry in which you work, your employees may have access to many different resources simply because they live across the country. University programs and other academic resources are becoming increasingly accessible online. Do some research and offer different opportunities to your staff based on your acquired knowledge of what makes them get out of bed in the morning. Make this an exciting opportunity to learn, grow, and expand whatever skill set they possess, and follow up with each of them regularly.

In a true hybrid model, if, for example, you and your staff are in the office 20 percent of the time, use that time specifically for intellectual stimulation and experimentation. Allow your people to dig into a project of their choosing, a course they want to take, or a new technology they want to explore, and then come back together at the end of the day or time together and discuss their ideas. Use this time to connect with and guide your people.

Inspirational Motivation

I have to say that this might be one of my favorite tenets of transformational leadership. Inspirational motivation refers to how the leader articulates a vision that is appealing and inspiring to followers. Inspirational motivation is vastly different from situational motivation. Situational motivation is fleeting and based on quickly changing circumstances. Inspirational motivation endures because it is based on the vision and mission that the team puts into place and has bought into.

A coach can try to motivate a ballplayer to win a baseball game, but once the ninth inning rolls around, their motivation changes from striking out the last hitter to the post-game pizza binge. If a coach is motivating a player to become a professional baseball player, the game literally and figuratively changes. The focus is no longer on the single game. It becomes something more. That coach's job is to inspire that player to work hard on and off the field, eat right, stay healthy, and do what he needs to do to help the team. This is what inspirational motivation is all about, and once again, it involves a leader getting to know his or her people.

Inspirational motivators—again, that's you—consistently challenge their people with high standards, are optimistic about future goals, and show their people the value and meaning of the work being done. If you want your people to act, you have to motivate them in ways other than salaries, bonuses, or other transactional benefits. What intrinsically drives your people to get up in the morning? What really gets their gears moving? Why do they want to be here? Actually, the main question here is, how in the world are leaders supposed to inspire and motivate their people through a computer screen or over the phone?

Vision casting and mission creation! It all starts with casting a vision and creating an organizational mission *with* your team. Vision casting and mission building can be difficult—even more so if you try to do it all alone. As you walk through this process with your team, what will surface are people's motivations, dreams, skill sets, ambitions, and so much more. You will be able to assess what inspirationally motivates each member of your team. Take notes because this information will be vital in successfully accomplishing the mission you and your team will create.

The great news here is that technology has paved the way for vision casting and mission creation to be done in a hybrid way. Take half a day and get your team's perspective on the issues they are seeing and how they want to move toward mission and vision creation. Use one of your "in-person" workdays to brainstorm with your team, and if necessary, set up a virtual room for those who can't be there in person.

At this point, your job is to drive the conversation and write down ideas. There are so many great ways to facilitate creating a vision: Strengths, Weaknesses, Opportunities, and Threats (SWOT) analysis, mind mapping, collaborative brainwriting, etc. All of these analysis techniques can be accomplished in person or in a virtual environment, but in any case, building your organizational vision with your team members will instill in them a sense of belonging and the belief that they can be certain their input was baked into the vision. You, in turn, will be able to identify the unique skill sets of your respective team members and will be able to use those to accomplish your mission.

After your team's vision and mission statement are set in stone, refer to them often. Start your meetings off this way, reminding your team that this is the result of their hard work. Once your vision is set, you can use what we've already learned from individual consideration and intellectual stimulation to move toward organizational change and long-term success, constantly communicating with your team about their needs and pointing them toward the established goal.

Idealized Influence

In the Marine Corps, our mantra was, "Do the right thing, even when you think no one is looking." Idealized influence refers to how you conduct yourself as a role model and leader of character in the boardroom, on a Zoom call, and after hours. A good leader conducts himself or herself in a manner worth following. This pertains to how they speak, listen, act, and respond to their employees' needs, concerns, and complaints.

We have all been on that Zoom call when someone forgets to mute themselves. We start to hear the chatter that seems to have nothing to do with the actual conversation. Everyone else stops talking and looks to see who has the "hot mic." If you are sitting at the virtual head of the table, you frantically search for the mute button to ensure that your team member doesn't embarrass themselves and that they don't say anything or have the team hear them say something they will regret.

This is an all-too-familiar occurrence these days. As leaders, we must live our lives, professionally and personally, as if our mute button is broken. The people we lead are watching us, listening to us, and analyzing our behavior. Leadership failures often bleed over into personal failures that could have been avoided. If you are to be trusted as a leader, you have to be holistically trustworthy.

Idealized influence can be tricky in hybrid work, where we don't often see each other outside of our daily interactions over the computer screen. This can either be used as an excuse for inappropriate leadership behavior, or it can be used as an accountability tool. The "do as I say and not as I do" model of leadership is what we are trying to combat here, and if we lead the way we want to be led in every aspect of our lives, we will eventually become the holistic leaders that will take our organizations, families, and peers to the next level of success.

We all have flaws and make mistakes. Even the great Steve Jobs sometimes made questionable leadership decisions. However, in a world where news and gossip travel instantaneously through social media networks, emails, and texts, we must ensure that our behavior is above reproach. When we do make mistakes, we must address them appropriately and quickly. The bottom line here for you is, you have to lead in a way that *you* would like to be led. Would you want *you* as your boss?

*

Transformational leadership theory is a fluid process of knowing and communicating with your people. What we have to focus on throughout the process of incorporating these four tenets is that we are focused on organizational enhancement through the enhancement of our people. You may find these processes to be too loose and not legalistic enough, but that's the point. If we, as leaders, are going to continue to steer our organizations toward success, it starts with the people. The main idea here is that if your people are nurtured toward creativity, growth, consideration, and motivation, your organization will be more creative, considerate, and motivated, and your growth will surpass your expectations.

So, as a leader, how do we wrap all of these tenets up into a nice package and actually use them? How do we rehumanize a dehumanized work environment? The foundation of this answer is to know who your people are, what makes them tick, and transform motivation into disciplined inspiration. But where do we even start? What happens when the entire organization has to change? Let's continue to dive into Traci's story and follow along as she walks her team and her organization through a transition into the hybrid world using Dr. John Kotter's eight-step methodology, but first, take a look at some Questions to Consider and Transformation Tips.

QUESTIONS TO CONSIDER

1. How do you organize your day? Are there things you can do in your home office to make the day better? Ask the same thing of your team.

2. What are some ways that you can help your team to feel individually considered?

3. How can you intellectually stimulate your people over a computer screen?

4. What inspirationally motivates you professionally? Why do you get up in the morning and go to work?

5. What does your ideal leader look like? How do *you* want to be led?

6. How can you get "buy-in" from your team regarding your organizational or team vision?

7. How can you use the tenets of transformational leadership theory to lead your hybrid or remote team?

TRANSFORMATION TIPS

1. Traditional nine-to-five jobs are rapidly becoming a thing of a past. Sometimes it's 9:00–11:00, 1:00–3:00, 5:00—7:00, and 10:24–10:30. If you try to manage everyone on your team's daily schedule, you will quickly overwhelm yourself.

TIP

Ensure that the work is being done (use or create metrics or standards of work), that your people have what they need, and that you are available when necessary. If there are requirements that need to be met throughout the day, make sure that these are addressed; otherwise, give the team some breathing room regarding their schedules. Studies show that a flexible work schedule is a top priority for remote employees and an inflexible schedule is a big reason why people leave careers.

2. Small talk is a part of life. It's also a part of any productive meeting. Talking about nonwork items breaks the ice and helps the leader transition into the meeting. In a hybrid environment, where you may have a mix of people online and in-person, small talk is still important.

TIP

From the get-go, make it a requirement that those online must have their cameras on if possible. There is nothing more impersonal than a computer screen filled with names and no faces. Not only will requiring this help to rehumanize the experience, but it will empower your virtual folks, at the very least, to put on a presentable shirt and comb their hair. This isn't about a dress code; it's about promoting self-care and helping your people to do the basics—and yes, this includes you. Another tip to increase engagement is to start the virtual meeting ten minutes early and end ten minutes later. These ten minutes aren't a requirement for attendance, but will provide the space for people to catch up before diving directly into business.

3. Again, culture eats strategy for breakfast. Without trust, you cannot lead a hybrid team (or any team, for that matter) or cultivate a transformational culture, but how can you build trust with your team over the phone?

TIP

Building trust should be a leader's top priority, and it's up to you as the leader, not your people. Here are some step-by-step recommendations for building trust through transformational leadership.

Be available and communicative: Your team needs to know, at the very least that you are available to them when they need you. This doesn't mean that you drop everything to accommodate—you have a job to do as well. What this does mean is that you respond to requests quickly and with the intent to follow through.

Follow through: The first time you don't follow through with one of your team members is the first time their trust in you begins to waver. Yes, we all forget things from time to time, but as you build up and maintain the trust of your hybrid team, following through with communication is dramatically important. Hybrid work has taken away the ability for your people to just pop in on you to remind you of something they requested. Yes, they can email or chat, but if you are responsive and follow through before you are reminded, your team will trust you even more.

Have fun!: Your people don't want to work for a robot. Working on a hybrid team can be isolating. Imagine that the majority of your "human" interactions were through a computer screen. Then imagine that the only thing you are talking about or doing during these interactions was work related. Put a lot of effort into making the day fun for your people. Hold contests, send prizes, and create an environment that your people want to be a part of. Intellectually stimulate your team in creative and new ways and make having fun part of that.

TWO

WHAT WOULD KOTTER DO

Unpacking the Eight Steps of Organizational Change

Humans are creatures of habit and structure. When we are given a problem, we look to the familiar, tried-and-true solution to help us solve it. If we can lean on processes and procedures to help us succeed, we will. Having a playbook that we can rely on when we need to institute change is truly an amazing thing to have, and Dr. John P. Kotter gives us that playbook in his book *Leading Change*.

John P. Kotter and his eight-step process for organizational change is a foundational tool for change. The eight steps are extremely useful when used against an issue like morphing an organization into a hybrid work environment. The eight-step process for leading change was refined over forty years from Kotter's observations of many different organizations and their leadership teams as they attempted to execute business strategies and change their organizations. So, without further ado, I give you Kotter's eight steps.

The Eight-Step Process for Leading Change

1. **Create a sense of urgency:** Motivate your people by making sure they understand why the organization is changing and why it has to be done quickly.
2. **Build a guiding coalition:** Building a coalition of supporters to help you institute change will give you the team you need to move forward, and quickly.
3. **Form strategic vision and initiatives:** Clarify how the future will be different from the past.
4. **Enlist a volunteer army:** This peer group will act as the brain trust for change. They will be your biggest cheerleaders, and you will be theirs.
5. **Enable action by removing barriers:** You are changing for a reason. Remove the old barriers, such as defunct processes and procedures, and promote opportunities to create new processes.
6. **Generate short-term wins:** Short-term goals will lead to short-term wins. Celebrating these wins will also keep your team motivated and moving quickly toward mission accomplishment.
7. **Sustain acceleration:** Once you have tasted success, keep pushing toward another achievement. Keep up the forward momentum and address setbacks in a positive way.
8. **Institute change:** Now it's time to show off! Show off your work and compare the outcome to what you came from.[1]

John P. Kotter is widely considered a leading organizational change expert. He and his team have made it their mission to walk alongside leaders and those instituting organizational change. Kotter understands the dynamics of change and how personal it can be. Kotter's eight-step plan has been one of the most useful tools in my toolbox throughout my organizational change journeys, and I can't think of a better way to address the organizational change that so many of us are going through in this shift toward hybrid work.

Now that we have identified and defined the steps, let's go back to the inspiring story of our friendly Director of Information And Technology (IT), Traci. Let's reconnect with her right after she's told her team that the company is going hybrid and see how she uses Kotter's eight-step process for leading change.

We last left Traci in the boardroom of her office building. She was notified by her boss that their company would be moving to a completely hybrid model of work and she has to figure out how to motivate her team to not only successfully operate within this new structure but thrive personally and professionally. Easy day, right?

Following the meeting where Traci broke the news to her team, she sent them home for the rest of the day to gather their thoughts and process what just happened. Even though Traci is in the boardroom alone, you can still feel the tension. It's like Florida humidity in the middle of the summer. It's heavy, and uncomfortable, and full of bugs… After a quick rotation of her neck and stretch of the back, she stands up and heads into her office to strategize. Her main job at this point is to make sure that her team can function and thrive through this change, so it's time to bring in the eight steps!

Step 1: Create a Sense of Urgency

John P. Kotter describes this sense of urgency: "A sense of urgency is a powerful tool for anyone wanting to win in a turbulent world that will only continue to move faster. Management control systems and damage control experts serve a critical purpose. But don't let that blind you to an increasingly important reality. Controls can support complacency in an era when complacency can be deadly."[2]

Given the post pandemic shift toward hybrid work, the urgency is already created. The problem is figuring out how to spin the sense of urgency into something positive. Traci heads into her office and starts to think out loud, "Okay, I have ten people to think of here. There is absolutely no way to make everyone 100 percent happy with the decisions I am going to have to make, so what are the best options? Business isn't stopping just because my team in turmoil, so I have to come up with a strategy, and quick."

Traci quickly confers with her boss, collecting all the details she needs to get this hybrid ball rolling. They quickly put together a plan for her team that will maintain the speed of business and at the same time put her people in a great position to succeed. The trick will be creating this same sense of urgency within her team.

She comes up with an action plan. Traci thinks best out loud, so as she paces, she says to herself, "Once everyone is comfortable working from home, we will need to have at least one workday where we are all together. Most of the team is actually excited that they get to work from home, and if we are all spread to the wind, it will be more and more difficult as time goes on to get everyone in the office."

Traci knows the importance of actual human interaction and builds time for this into her hybrid plan. Her team will come into the office one day a week, half on Wednesdays and half on Fridays. During these in-person office days, the team will strategize how to stay ahead of the competition and create a new vision for what their team will look like and accomplish. Traci's game plan will quickly uncover any fears, problems, ideas, issues, and preferences of her team members. These "in-person" days will be used to ensure that the team understands the urgency of getting back in the batter's box, or back in business, and continue to hit grand slams. She gets them engaged, involved, and bought into the process. This builds directly toward the next step—building a guiding coalition.

Step 2: Build a Guiding Coalition

Executive Champion: If you are going to transition your team successfully into a nimble, highly productive beast of a team in your new hybrid work environment, you are going to need some very specific people in your corner. Due to the sensitivity of Traci's transition, the first member of her coalition, she decides, should be a senior representative of the company. The person filling this role acts as the sponsor for change, Traci's top cover, and your team's advocate to other seniors. Top cover refers to a leader's requirement to go to bat for their team and to ensure that the team is taken care of. He or she will be the team champion, providing the team with the logistical and executive-level support needed to implement change.

Peer Supporters: Not only is top cover necessary, but support from Traci's peers will also be a pivotal part of this shift.

Trusted peer supporters act as a sounding board and as advisors throughout the shift from on-site to hybrid work. Traci is going to need to pull together other leaders at her level to work toward the change goal. In this case, her peers are going through the same change, so this will be a group of individuals with similar visions, missions, and goals. Traci will have to lean on this group when things get rough—and they will.

The Team: These are Traci's direct reports or those in similar roles as those of her direct reports. They believe in the mission and vision and not only are willing to work toward them but are their champions among the company. Traci will rely on her team to do their day-to-day jobs as well as to assist in the transition to hybrid work and to champion the process overall.

The Coalition: This entity is composed of the entire coalition of supporters. This group is a conglomerate of senior leaders, peers, and team members who have bought into the change and are ready to hold each other accountable for instituting the change. Traci must outline each of the cohorts' responsibilities and roles, but the movement toward mission accomplishment and vision actualization is the main goal of this group.

Step 3: Form Strategic Vision and Initiatives

Okay, Traci has assembled her coalition and it's time to get to work! Vision casting is the most important part of this plan and must be done quickly, so she sends an invite to her internal team. They will get together via videoconference for a full week in order to establish through two separate missions.

The first is the business vision. How will they continue to thrive in a fast-paced, dog-eat-dog business and maintain their scalability in this new hybrid work environment? How can she transform her team into a hybrid powerhouse that doesn't skip a beat in the successful completion of their jobs? Traci gathers up the forecasted business needs and deadlines and sends them to the team. Throughout the week, they will either confirm that their current vision and strategies are still valid, or they will create new ones that align to their new work environment.

The second vision, which I argue is the more important of the two, is the vision they will cast for how they will operate as a team. What will their work schedules look like? What resources do they need *now* to overcome this mountainous challenge quickly? How do they keep morale high and the team cohesive? I say that this vision is most important because it will directly impact Traci's team's ability to accomplish the company's mission and move in line with its vision.

Step 4: Enlist a Volunteer Army

Traci's next task is to assemble her previously identified peer team; however, her volunteer army will serve in a different role than her guiding coalition identified in step 2. This army of volunteers will be the brain trust of the transformation. What I mean by *brain trust* is that this team will help the direct team, executive team, and the entire organization create procedures for change and promote the positive change these procedures will bring. This group is her voice to the rest of the company to help get others to buy into her organizational change philosophy.

As Traci sets up her army, she identifies leaders across her organization who are in similar situations. The entire organization is moving hybrid, so there are plenty of fellow leaders out there in need of this type of mutual support. Knowing this, Traci reaches out to her peer group (her army) and schedules weekly meetings with them, outlining her ideas, current processes, projected processes, and questions to be answered. This army will work together to share best practices within the entire organization and help it transition and act as the infantry men and women for institutional change.

Step 5: Enable Action by Removing Barriers

A barrier is simply something that's in your way, slowing down your journey to your final destination. In this case, Traci must remove some of the mental barriers her team and organization are concerned with. With her volunteer army in formation, she begins highlighting barriers and action plans to address each obstacle. Here are just a few barriers Traci will run into.

Barrier 1: Fear. Fear is a universal barrier associated with any change. With change comes excitement, nerves, and often times fear. Traci's team has been told that their entire mode of work life will have to change. The first step in helping her team overcome the fear of this uncertainty goes back to the first concept of transformational leadership: individual consideration.

During Traci's scheduled one-on-one meetings with each member of her team, several different items were discussed. First, how are they doing with the announcement? What are their thoughts about hybrid work? What are they afraid of, and most of all, how can she help them overcome their fears?

Second, Traci must reassure her team that they will be taken care of logistically, technologically, and personally. Traci will ensure that they have what they need to succeed, and if their needs ever change, she will be there to address those needs—not necessarily to accommodate every need, but to be there to listen to and understand the need. She's not there to oblige every request, but she is there to make sure that her team has everything they need to be successful.

Finally, Traci must ensure that her team members are continuously aligned with the two visions (their business vision and their team vision). Since the entire team contributed to the crafting of these visions, it's Traci's job to make sure that as they remove barriers, they are still sprinting toward these visions and continuing to contribute to the success of the company.

Barrier 2: Communication Gaps. As in any relationship, good and consistent communication is vital. Even in a traditional work setting where everyone is in the office, communication is challenging. Throw in remote employees, and you dramatically increase communication barriers and the importance of trust.

Communication is going to look dramatically different as Traci's team transitions. She is going to have to draw some lines in the sand by answering some basic but important questions. Will there be a requirement to have cameras on during meetings? Will she be willing to have the virtual open-door policy, where she is always available to her team? How will she address the topic of accountability? Here's what she decides to do.

Traci sets up her "virtual open-door policy" on day one. This will allow her team to contact her at any given time throughout the day. This policy is Traci's way of letting her team know that she is there for them when they need her. What this policy is *not* is a tether to her computer. As a leader helping to transition an entire organization into a hybrid one while at the same time continuing to grow her business and lead her people, she has a full plate.

Traci decides that for the first three weeks her virtual room will be open for six hours a day—three hours in the morning and three hours in the afternoon. After the first three months, if the needs of her team slow down, she will then only have her room open for three hours in the morning, but she will still be available when she isn't otherwise occupied.

Barrier 3: Accountability Issues. Accountability is another challenge that Traci has to tackle head on. There is no clock to punch and minimal in-person accountability measures, so Traci must rely on trust and an intensified focus on the business metrics themselves. Traci is able to give her team specific short-term goals to focus on and achieve. Each of these short-term goals is in line with mission accomplishment and tied to their team's vision, so as these goals are achieved, the business will grow.

If the business continues to grow, accountability must be in place. The last thing Traci wants to do is hold her team to a strict work schedule, but if the business begins to tank, that's exactly what she'll have to do. In the meantime, she will give her team the flexibility they need to adjust to their new work world and everything they need to succeed in hybrid work life.

There are many other barriers that Traci may run into, but fears, communication challenges, and accountability issues are a few barriers that other obstacles often stem from. We will discuss some of the other barriers at the end of this chapter in the Questions to Consider section.

Step 6: Generate Short-Term Wins

I know, we essentially have already talked in steps 1 through 5 about generating short-term wins—i.e., the concept of creating micro-goals as you work toward the broader goal of mission success—but let's take it a step further, diving into why short-term wins are so important for successful organizational change. We talked about how short-term goals and wins were important for Traci's team, but how can Traci align her professional goals with those of the broader team? Here's how Traci organizes her short-term goals by working backward from her team's mission and vision statements.

First, Traci establishes her business goals. These are the goals that will keep her on track regarding successfully growing her business. She looks at the necessary metrics from the year prior and breaks them down into monthly chunks. This will help her to stay on top of the business and will force her to maintain focus on growth and the success of the organization.

Second, Traci sets up milestones for transforming her organization and team. Again, these are monthly goals, which will include collecting data from her team, her volunteer army, and her executive champion. Each month she outlines her goals, progress, and questions she needs to answer or have answered. Communication is key here. She has to communicate her goals and attainment plan with the entire coalition, and having monthly check-ins and goals will keep the transformation moving forward, keeping everyone involved informed about the process.

Finally, Traci plans to *celebrate*! What is the point of generating short-term wins without celebrating and acknowledging them? This is one of the most important parts of this process, not only for Traci but for the entire coalition. In order to make sure that the entire coalition feels celebrated, Traci sets up the last Friday of each month as a celebration day! This is a time for the entire coalition to come together, virtually or in person (their choice), and celebrate the great work they have done over the past month, and to look toward what they will be celebrating during their next monthly meeting. Celebrating these wins and planning for the future sets up the next step in the process.

Step 7: Sustain Acceleration

In business, if you aren't accelerating, you are dying. As Traci moves into this step of the process, she has undoubtedly faced monumental challenges and setbacks. Just because Kotter has outlined eight steps for leading change doesn't mean it will be a smooth journey. As with any change, there will be unforeseen challenges that can slow down acceleration, but it is Traci's job, as the leader of her team and an essential part of her organization, to maintain forward momentum and solidify new concepts and processes before they fade into the distance.

Each of Kotter's eight-step process for leading change is built upon the last. Up to this point, Traci has created a sense of urgency and need within her team and organization, built her coalition of executives, peers, and team members, created a change vision and formed strategic initiatives, enlisted her army, addressed and removed barriers, and generated her short-term goals and wins. Now it's time to sew these accomplishments into the organizational fabric of hybrid work.

As Traci begins to implement work schedules, project due dates, goals, short-term wins, and acceleration strategies, she makes sure to record and analyze failures and successes. Some of the questions running through her mind are, *What is working? What's absolutely not working? Can we do this better? Is what we are doing sustainable?* As she answers these questions, Traci is formalizing repeatable policies and setting up the structure in which her team and organization will work for the foreseeable future. With the assumption that this new hybrid work model is here to stay, she begins to institutionalize her successes and reassess her failures.

Step 8: Institute Change

Last but definitely not least, Traci must institutionalize the change. Again, building off the previous steps, this step is where it all comes together. At this point, Traci and her team have been operating in a hybrid working environment for some time now. Traci has ironed out the wrinkles in her scheduling plan, she's been able to accelerate her business, and the team is satisfied with their routines. Now is the time to bring her best practices to her coalition and the executive team in order to implement the change throughout the company and show them how to do it!

*

We've walked with Traci through her version of using Kotter's eight steps to change her organization into a hybrid one. This is just one example of how this can be done, but the meat and potatoes behind Kotter's eight steps remain the same. As we change our organizations, whether into a hybrid model of work or through any other large-scale change, these steps can be used as a guide for successful implementation of change.

To recap just a bit, when leading change, we must create a sense of urgency for everyone involved. This will help to light a fire under those in charge who are implementing the change. After we've communicated the necessity for urgency, we need to build up our support group who will help us do this right. As we put the coalition of supporters in place, we craft our strategies and vision for the change—in this case, operating an organization in a hybrid work environment. Then we get to work by enlisting the help of others who are impacted by this change, all moving toward a common goal. Barriers are inevitable in any work environment. Hybrid work adds but also takes away barriers that we as leaders will have to identify, and as we remove certain barriers, we have to stop and celebrate their destruction. Sustainment of the success we've already had will build the foundation of institutional change. As we build this airplane in the air, we must make sure that we screw on the steering wheel and that it doesn't get taken off. Finally, we have to institutionalize this change by ensuring buy-in from the coalition.

Once these steps are achieved, you are off to the races, set up for success and continued acceleration. However, the completion of the eight steps doesn't mean that you won't have to go back to the drawing board. It doesn't mean that you'll never encounter leadership challenges within your new environment that won't require contingencies and plans B, C, and D. Now, let's walk through what we can do when the proverbial stuff hits the fan and your leadership skills are put to the test in an uncomfortable and stressful environment of contingency. Take a look at the Questions to Consider and Transformation Tips sections below, and then we'll dive into a story about contingency in an environment that we may not all be familiar with:

It was Afghanistan 2010 . . .

QUESTIONS TO CONSIDER

1. For you, what are some of the top-of-mind things to prioritize when you have to lead change?

2. Which of Kotter's eight steps do you feel would be most helpful?

3. How would you use the steps in your specific organizational change journey?

4. Have you surrounded yourself (virtually or otherwise) with the right people? How can you enhance your team?

5. What role, if any, are you missing in the composition of your coalition or volunteer army? How might you be able to incorporate this role in the future?

TRANSFORMATION TIPS

1. I realize that organizational change isn't always a common leadership challenge. Many organizations have been operating in this hybrid world for quite some time.

TIP:

Use Kotter's eight steps as a guide for team building and sustainment. As you build or sustain the momentum of your team, continue to find people around you who can help you lead. This takes courage, confidence, and a good amount of humility, but years from now, when your coalition is filled with people who will speak wisdom, provide encouragement, and hold you accountable, you will find that the leadership journey becomes much easier. In a hybrid environment, your reach is boundless. Use the tools available to you to build up your coalition and lean on them when things get hard—because they will.

2. Kotter's eight steps are difficult to get accomplished in a hybrid work world. You can't just pop into the next office and brainstorm with a colleague. Difficult, yes. Impossible, absolutely not!

TIP:

Since you are dealing with hybrid teams, your organizational skills are going to play a key role in your success. Be deliberate in each step and make sure you follow through. Building, changing, and sustaining teams can't be accomplished without a well thought out plan. For example, when you are measuring goals and celebrating wins, you must communicate these goals to your team clearly and empower them, leading them toward accomplishing these goals. Present your team with your expectations and show them what success looks like. But remember, rarely is a plan executed exactly the way you've laid it out. Be ready to have contingencies and be willing to lean on your team and your coalition.

THREE

CONTINGENCY LEADERSHIP
What Happens When the Stuff Hits the Fan

The strangely satisfying smell of a sandstorm that has been overwhelmed by a sudden and unexpected torrential downpour is as unique an experience as there is, rivaled only by the sight of it. Watching this magnificent mountain of sand, dancing and fighting to stay alive against an overpowering rainstorm, was like watching the Almighty engage in fierce and absolute combat with the devil himself. *Ah, Afghanistan. I might miss you, just a tiny bit,* I thought to myself.

Over the past seven months in Helmand Province, Afghanistan, my fellow Marines and I had been on several missions where the objective was clear and the outcome was relatively predictable. We would help the locals plant grain in place of poppy, hunt for Taliban fighters in tiny towns in southern Helmand Province, and confiscate and destroy narcotics coming from the south. At times, it felt eerily identical to our Iraq deployment from the previous year. This mission, however, was anything but predictable or routine.

The fresh rain falling from the swirling black clouds was inundating the reddish brown sandstorm billowing from the south, filling the air with an orange tint and a smell that can only be described as one of the most refreshing, yet overpowering, sensations one human sense can experience. It was literally raining mud. Powerful thunder and penetrating lightning overstimulated every nerve in my body. The terrain of Afghanistan had to be the only place on Earth where this phenomenon was possible, and I was able to experience it from the turret of a fully armored vehicle amongst U.S. Marine Corps brothers whom I would never forget.

My machine gun locked to the rear, ready to take on whatever was sent my way, and our four-vehicle convoy had been halted due to the pending sandstorm, in preparation to travel through a narrow, IED-laden mountain pass (IEDs are Improvised Explosive Devices). Before the rain started, we battened down the hatches and prepared to get pounded by the commanding sandstorm as we had been several times over the past few months. We watched this larger-than-life scene play out in front of us, knowing that once it was safe to move, we were headed into a part of Afghanistan that very few Western militaries had ever been.

We knew that we were headed toward a firefight with the Taliban, and we knew that our route was already mapped out by the enemy and laced with IEDs. Nevertheless, after about forty-five minutes of watching and waiting, the convoy commander sounded over the radio that it was time to move out. This meant we had about five to ten minutes before we would start our journey through the mountains of southern Helmand Province, down a single lane dirt "road." We had no idea what to expect.

Every contingency imaginable was going through my head. How do you plan if you don't know what's going to happen?

Our destination was one of the few remaining Taliban strongholds in Helmand, in a town split by the Pakistan-Afghanistan border. There was one road in and one road out. The problem was that we didn't have access to the one road out. It was in Pakistan, and we were given strict orders to stay out unless we wanted to be the reason for an international incident. We really didn't want that to happen.

As we started checking our communication gear and made sure our ammunition was readily available, what we were about to do really hit home. The unknown became doubt, which turned into fear. Would I make it home? Was my new wife going to receive nothing but a folded flag and a letter from a thankful nation?

I felt nervous, nauseous, and scared all at once, but I couldn't show it. I wasn't anywhere near the senior Marine in the convoy, but I was the senior Marine in the vehicle, and at the very least I had to look like I could lead these Marines and our navy corpsmen down this road. While my nerves were on the verge of getting the best of me, my face was still, and my trigger finger was ready. After checking my weapon and giving a quick "Ooh-rah" to my Marines, I sat back, closed my eyes, said a prayer, and began to plan.

As I thought about all the potential outcomes that may play out over the next forty-eight hours, the magnitude of what my decisions could cost hit home like a bullet to the flak jacket. I looked at my Marines, and I knew that my main objective was to keep them alive. The unit's mission objective was to take over a Taliban stronghold and narcotic bazaar. This place was responsible for killing three of our Marines in the months prior and an original source of deadly heroin trafficked throughout Europe, Russia, and Asia.

Many of the homemade explosives that killed U.S. Marines throughout Helmand Province came from this bazaar. Our mission was, at the very least, to put a dent in their operation. In that moment, my personal mission was put into perspective. The reality and weight of the consequences of poor decision making became tangible. I had to be flexible in my decision making, able to shift my thought process and leadership style depending on what the situation called for.

The American military hierarchy is built upon orders and a chain of command for a reason—because it works. In that moment, I knew I could rely on that "structure" to lead, but at the end of the day the structure is only as good as the leader in command of it. I had to find a fluid balance between hierarchy and humanity to get my Marines through this mountain pass and to keep my stuff together—idealized influence.

I was jolted back into the present by the starting of my vehicle's diesel engine, smoke billowing out of the back tailpipes and into the turret in which I was mounted. The convoy commander gave the command, and we moved out, following right behind the rain.

The rain had put an end to the massive sandstorm and turned the road into a trail of thick red mud, forcing the convoy to move more slowly than we would have liked, but we pushed on toward our objective. From the turret of the last vehicle, I could see the entire countryside behind the convoy. The vast sandy dessert quickly met the rocky and treacherous mountains of Southern Afghanistan, and as we headed into the mountain pass, I noticed something. Small pieces of broken wood, multicolored wires, and plastic jugs were beginning to surface on either side of our convoy.

The rain was still very heavy in front of us, making the roads a muddy mess, but not a drop fell on us. After passing the third set of what I now recognized as IED components, the convoy came to another stop. The convoy commander came over the radio asking for our Explosives Ordinate Disposal (EOD) Sergeant to dismount and figure out what was going on. The EOD Sergeant knew what the pieces were immediately but agreed to investigate. We shifted the vehicles into a defensive posture and settled in for what we thought would be a while.

After a few minutes of visually clearing the area for Taliban fighters, the EOD Sergeant dismounted and headed toward a particular set of wires. Metal detector in hand, he swept the area for IEDs and quickly hit pay dirt. Directly under the wires and busted-up wood was a fifty-pound yellow jug of homemade explosives, which would have demolished our vehicle and every United States Marine and Navy Corpsman in it. Once he marked the jug, he moved on to investigate the wires. He opened his multi tool—i.e., basically a pair of needle nose pliers with several other attachments on it—and sorted through the mess.

When it seemed like he had conducted a thorough investigation, he quickly stood up, moved back to the truck, and jumped in the first vehicle. After only a few seconds of discussion, the convoy commander came over the radio. "The rain completely destroyed the IEDs on our path. We actually ran over three of them before we got to this one. Whoever was praying for a miracle on this operation, keep it up!"

The rain had destroyed the wood the Taliban was using as an initiator for the IEDs. I heard an audible gasp from my Marines in the vehicle, looking to me for leadership and guidance. With a new sense of security and burst of confidence, I looked down from the turret, smirked, and gave them a look that said, "Let's do this." They all nodded back without saying a word. Our plans changed. Now it was time to get to work. It's amazing how stress can bring out the best or the worst in you. Throughout that mission, I continuously had to change my plans based on whatever situation we were faced with.

The great philosopher Mike Tyson once said, "Everyone has a plan until they get punched in the mouth." I'll speak for myself here, but sometimes life and leadership can deliver blows to the stomach, the mouth, legs, head, and sometimes the back. Leading people is hard, largely due to the ever-changing circumstances we are faced with as leaders. One day you're able to provide your staff with all the intellectual stimulation they need, and the next, you are all hands on deck trying to meet a deadline that was just moved up by a month. We all have our plans and a particular way that we like to lead, but if life has taught us nothing else, it's that we have to be able to adapt to changing circumstances, even in the most painful and unimaginable of situations.

Contingency leadership is based on the principle that a leader's effectiveness is contingent on whether their leadership style suits a particular situation. I am going to push back against this definition and offer a broader spectrum of contingency. In my opinion, the ability for a leader to adapt and adjust their leadership style based on the current situation at hand is not only necessary, but it's vital for success and growth. The good news here is that it can be taught and done well. Let's dive into how contingency leadership can be used in hybrid leadership and look at some tangible steps to help us become more flexible leaders.

Let's start with one of the major contributors to the field of contingency leadership, Dr. Fred Edward Fiedler. Fiedler's research on contingent leadership "puts forth the idea that effective leadership hinges not only on the style used by the leader, but also on the control held over the situation."[1] Dr. Fiedler, who held a PhD in psychology, spearheaded some of the most groundbreaking research on industrial and organizational psychology. Some say that he revolutionized organizational psychology, helping to shape the industry for generations to come. He is famously quoted for saying that "the quality of leadership, more than any other single factor, determines the success or failure of an organization." Dr. Fiedler was also affectionately honored with the title of "the man who napped" by his family. According to his daughter, Dr. Fiedler had a special chair in which he would doze off in the afternoons for over twenty years. Dr. Fiedler was truly a man who knew the importance of rest.[2]

In 1997 Dr. Fiedler published one of his last articles for the United States Army Research Institute for the Behavioral and Social Sciences titled "Leadership Experience and Organizational Performance," in which he summarized twenty years of research on cognitive resources and organizational performance. Dr. Fiedler defined "cognitive resources" as intellectual abilities, job-relevant technical knowledge, and experience. Within the first two paragraphs of the report, Fiedler throws down the leadership gauntlet:

The research which is reported here investigated
over 1,100 leaders from a wide variety of military,
para-military, and civilian organizations, as well as
leaders who participated in laboratory experiments.
*Almost invariably, an experience from which one has
"really learned" occurred in association with stressful or
anxiety-arousing conditions. In return, in emergencies,
stressful conditions, or crises, there is frequently little
time to think, and responses to these conditions tend to
be automatic, and based on experience and overlearned
behavior.* Hence, there is strong emphasis on drill and
experience in such emergency-response organizations
as fire departments, military combat units, or
emergency medical teams. (emphasis added)[3]

This highlights how Fiedler felt about leadership and
how his research shaped what we call contingency theory.
Fiedler's research is grounded in the concept that there is no
one best leadership style or practice. In fact, Fiedler's research
is based upon the idea that leadership effectiveness is based
on the situation and how a leader reacts to various stressful
situations.

As leaders, we are faced with different challenges every
day. Some days may seem like Groundhog Day with repetitive
meetings that could have been emails, but how do we react
when the proverbial stuff hits the fan? Whether we are leading
remote, hybrid, or on-site teams, here's something I learned
in the Marine Corps that has helped me to navigate stressful
leadership challenges. It's called a five-paragraph order, or
SMEAC: Situation, Mission, Execution, Administration and

logistics, Command and Control (or Communication). Yes, of course it's an acronym.

SMEAC is a common military reporting mechanism for planning and contingency planning. It provides a structure through which a leader can assess a situation, but of course, I'm going to change it up a bit to fit our narrative to give you a step-by-step plan for when contingency leadership becomes necessary, but first, let's lay out a scenario through which we can work.

You have been successfully leading a hybrid computer software and hardware sales team for three years and your organization is thriving. Your sales team is killing it, you've achieved a state of hypergrowth for the year, your boss is ecstatic about the results, and your team morale is high. Your team's mission—"To provide above-and-beyond value to our customers through service, growth, and a people-first approach"—has been accomplished. The fiscal year is over, and you can't help but throw yourself back into your office chair, take a deep breath, and smile. Life is good.

It's time for a well-deserved break from the grind of sales and leadership, so you grab your family and take them to Florida—it's February in Colorado, so this makes sense! All you want is eighty-degree weather and a pool. So, you and your crew jump on a plane and take off. You turn your phone off, put on your noise-canceling headphones, close your eyes, and off you go into a state of slumber that can only be rivaled by a medical sedative.

The plane lands, and you can feel the warmth of the air just by looking out the window. The vision of snow-packed roads is replaced by palm trees and board shorts—but then you turn your phone back on . . .

Situation

Ding . . . Ding . . . Ding . . . Ding . . . Ding . . . You have
ten voice mails, twenty-three emails, and fifteen frantic text
messages filled with capital letters and exclamation points. As
you begin to sort through the wave of desperation, you discover
that supply chain issues have dramatically halted the shipment
of hardware to your biggest client, and in your inbox is an
email from the client company's Director of Information And
Technology, Traci (remember her?).

Dear Sir,

> It has come to my attention that the deadline for
> delivery of services has come and gone. Our company
> has been doing business with you for over fifteen years,
> and this is highly disappointing. The implications of
> this delay are detrimental to our projected growth for
> the first quarter of our fiscal year. If this issue is not
> fixed within the next three weeks, we will have no
> other option but to request that we be refunded for
> our purchase and take our business to another vendor.
> I look forward to your reply.

Respectfully,
Traci
Director, Information and Technology

This is a big deal. The order from Traci's company makes
up 75 percent of your revenue attained for the fiscal year. If

this deal is refunded, your team won't receive their projected commission, you will lose your biggest client, and you could face the potential of losing your team and even your job. Your vacation was just put on hold until you can figure out what to do. So, you take your family to the hotel, explain the situation, and this part is very important—take yourself off "Paid Time Off" (PTO) status. Time to get to work!

The first thing you need to do in assessing the situation is take a minute to catch your breath. Jumping into it without thinking things through will only set you back, so take a deep breath, go for a walk without your phone, figure out how you are going to communicate to your team and your boss, and just breathe. This doesn't have to take all day, but it should take more than five minutes. Once you feel like your blood pressure has lowered and you have some clarity on how you will begin, craft your game plan. As you focus on crafting your game plan, you must make sure that your team mission is continuously at the front of your mind.

Mission

Think about your mission as the paddle in a game of paddle ball. For those unfamiliar with this fantastic game of repetition, paddle ball consists of a wooden paddle, an elastic string, and a rubber ball. The point of the game is to hit the ball, which is secured to the paddle by the elastic string, with the paddle as many times as you can without missing. Trust me, it's exhilarating and hours of fun.

What I mean by considering the paddle your mission, is that you must always come back to the team's mission as the foundation of your decision making. In this case, all your ideas, plans, and initiatives must be tethered to your team's mission to "provide above-and-beyond value to our customers through service, growth, and a people-first approach." As you start to figure out how to solve this problem and communicate with your team, your strategy will be based on accomplishing the mission. You know what you have to do, and it all starts with mission execution.

Execution

Now that you've taken a few deep breaths and refocused on your mission, it's time to rally the troops—or at least their skill sets. How are you going to execute what needs to be done using the team you have? The execution stage is one of the most important pieces to SMEAC because this is where you use the understanding of your team's strengths to get the job done. Remember, each of your team members brings a unique skill set and talents that can be used to solve this problem. Think about the problem and begin dissecting it to play to the strengths of your team. Here's an example.

Michael is an expert on supply chain issues and has a knack for getting hardware and materials from point A to point B in record time. He will be responsible for determining the supply chain issue. As he navigates the problems and solves them, you must provide him the top cover he needs to be able to get the job done.

Julia is an amazing sales representative. She won the deal in the first place and has an excellent relationship with

Traci, the Director of IT. She will be your go-to person for any communication with Traci and will help to overcome any relational hurdles that come into play.

Jen is a master at documentation. You will need Jen to organize the spreadsheets, order logs, and create any other forms of written communication necessary to document progress. As you begin to solve this issue with the team, Jen will be documenting everything to ensure that it is legal, ethical, and mission centered.

John is your engineer and knows more about the hardware than anyone in the company. While the supply chain issues are being solved, he will maintain contact with Traci's engineers by giving them product updates and assurances that they have the best of the best working toward fixing this problem.

Ian is the vice president of procurement, and your boss. Yes, your boss is part of the execution phase. Ian is invited to every meeting and is the voice of your company to Traci and to his boss, the CEO of your company. He will provide top cover for you and your team as you get the job done.

Finally, there's you. You are to ensure that your team is moving toward mission accomplishment. You set the pace, establish deadlines, and give your team the space they need to fix the problem. Lead! That's your job. Give your team the tools they need to be successful. Help where it is needed, guide when it is necessary, and push when it is critical. Ultimately, *you* are responsible for the success of this mission, but your team is who will get you there. Don't forget to give credit where credit is due. Celebrate small wins and coach when necessary. This is where you literally make your money!

Administration and Logistics

In this scenario, this area is where the whole thing went wrong in the first place. Now that you have a plan for your team, you need to go back to the logistical drawing board. As you begin to walk through the execution phase, take the time to assess what your team will need to get the job done within the three-week time frame Traci has given you. Your team is spread across the country, so regular check-ins are difficult, and the open-door policy looks a bit different.

Intentionality and consistency are what will get you through this. Be intentional about checking in with your people. One best practice that I have used with remote teams in the past was to leave a virtual meeting room open for the entire workday. As a leader, you are logged in the entire time and are available to your team for any reason at any time throughout the day. Intentionality during times of high stress and contingency is extremely important. Regardless of whether you are in a virtual or in-person work environment, you must make sure that you are present and responsive.

In the Marine Corps, we had what was called a battle rhythm. This rhythm was our way of ensuring that our efforts were calculated and efficient as we worked toward mission accomplishment. It was a way to ensure consistency and order in chaotic environments. As it pertains to administration and logistics, a battle rhythm is a road map that keeps everything on track. Tasks like schedules, meeting times, goals, and daily lists of to-dos are all part of the battle rhythm. Logistically and administratively, setting up this battle rhythm for your team will help guide you toward success. Maybe this involves two check-ins with the team per day, or it may mean several one-on-one meetings throughout the week with a team meeting at the end of the week. As the leader of this remote team, establish consistent touchpoints and deadlines. Believe it or not, your team craves this type of regimen, especially in a hybrid working environment. Furthermore, when you are operating in a high-stress and ambiguous environment, this structure will make accountability and success measurement more attainable.

Command and Control

Command and control are military terms meant to encompass the leadership structure through which a mission will be accomplished. In our scenario, command and control is where the leadership rubber meets the leadership road. As the leader of this team, this supply chain problem is your responsibility. Remember, this deal made up most of your income for the previous fiscal year, and the success or failure of its remediation is your responsibility.

The ability to take control of ambiguous situations is a difficult but necessary part of leadership. You are the leader of this team. You were hired because you not only know this business, but you have outstanding leadership skills. If you didn't, they would have selected someone else. Take ownership of this identity! Use it to rally, inspire, and motivate your team. Take command of this problem, and take pride in the work you and your team are doing. Organize the team in a way that utilizes their skills and gets the job done—and when the job is done, give the credit away! That's right, give the credit to your team and the work they have done. That's what being a leader is all about.

*

Let's tie a bow on this lesson on contingency leadership through the given scenario. You know the situation: your team must mend this relationship and exceed Traci's already tarnished expectations. After a thirty-minute jog, you have a good idea how to tackle this thing while sticking closely to your team's mission. You send the family to the beach and begin to organize your plan so that it is clear before presenting it to your boss and then your team. You identify the roles and responsibilities for which each member of your team will be responsible, you outline a communication plan that will keep your team on track, and you identify the desired outcome of your team's work.

Your first call is to your boss, outlining everything you have in mind. You get your marching orders and the clear message that this is the highest priority item in your job jar. Now it's time to communicate with the team. They are all aware of the discrepancy, and it's now your job to calm everyone down, organize them, and motivate them to succeed. An email is sent out to the entire team with their responsibilities clearly laid out, a link to the open meeting room, a schedule of deadlines, and the desired outcome of their work. Everything is in place . . . at least for now.

Contingency leadership is all about instituting structure and calm in an environment that is inherently unstructured and chaotic. Regardless of whether you are leading a team on-site, remotely, or hybrid, you will face leadership challenges that will push you outside your comfort zone. That's leadership in a nutshell. The ability to overcome adversity is a skill that must be sharpened and refined, but that only comes with the presence of adversity and the experience of working through it.

With a well-established structure to fall back on, these scenarios can become less of a crisis and more of a challenge that you and your team can attack with confidence. Technological advancements have made managing hybrid and remote teams administratively easier; however, leadership is a very personal job and requires more than just access to team members; it requires knowing your team's strengths and setting them up for success.

We talked at length about how to lead a team through a crisis and abrupt change, but how do we, as leaders, gain a deep understanding of our people? The people we lead aren't simply tools in a toolbox to be used on the latest task. Instead, all of our people are individuals with amazing backgrounds, histories, stories, and skills that they have accumulated over a lifetime of experiences. We must understand our people in order to put them in positions to succeed, but how do we do that? Let's dive into Dr. Urie Bronfenbrenner's model of ecological systems (I promise you will love it) and dissect an amazing tool for learning about our people and how they make decisions. Be sure to work through the following Questions to Consider and Transformation Tips first.

QUESTIONS TO CONSIDER

1. Do you know what your default leadership style is?

2. Take a good look at how you operate in a crisis. Do you have people to lean on when the stuff hits the fan?

3. What does your planning process look like? Is there room in this process for contingencies?

4. Take a look at your organization and your team structure. Have you identified places where single points of failure exist? In other words, are there systems in place where, when one person is eliminated from the equation, the whole system falls apart? What are they?

5. How can you eliminate these single points of failure?

6. What are some of your natural strengths and weaknesses? How can you address these and use them to deal well with contingency situations?

TRANSFORMATION TIPS

1. A single point of failure is an area within your team or organization that if a single person or entity were to fail, the damage would be significant. Eliminating single points of failure is essential for team building and sustainment and will drastically assist you in times of professional crisis.

> ## TIP:
>
> Take a good look at your priorities as an organization and what roles people fill to address these priorities. If you identify critical areas that aren't covered by more than one system or person, you have to put systems in place that will decrease the likelihood of failure if something goes wrong.

2. The story presented in this chapter is about contingencies when a process or business problem arises. What wasn't addressed is when an employee fails, causing a failure. How do you address the deeply personal situation of employee discipline? *This*, friends, is the core of leadership. How do you address employee problems in a healthy way? How do you individually consider your people but at the same time focus on what's best for the company? Furthermore, how on earth are you supposed to handle discipline in a hybrid or completely remote environment? This could be an entire book's worth of information, but hopefully this helps.

TIP:

When you signed up to lead, you signed up to coach. Coaching should be a big part of your leadership walk with your people. Coaching will help guide them through difficult work tasks, handling success, and addressing failure, and will provide them tools to succeed. Furthermore, when you have to discipline, you already have a place to start. "Mr. Employee, you are great at x-y-z. The issue here is with a-b-c. Let's see how we can use what we've been walking through to address a-b-c, using the strengths we've identified in x-y-z." Now, don't get me wrong: there are several examples of egregious failures that have to be addressed with negative consequence, possibly including termination of employment. That's just a fact. However, when possible, coaching your people through their failures will benefit the employee, yourself, and the organization, and will empower that employee to move forward instead of backward.

FOUR

UNDERSTANDING
THE INDIVIDUAL
Inside Our Decision-Making Process

One of my favorite tenets of transformational leadership is individual consideration. You must consider the individuals working for you in order to understand how to best lead and inspirationally motivate them. Your people are unique, have different and complementary skill sets, and are individually wired to learn, receive feedback, and be stimulated.

Leadership in remote and hybrid environments must start with the individual. In a disconnected culture, the more connected leaders are to their people, the better off their business and culture will be. However, to know your people, you must understand their worldviews and where they came from, learn how and why they make decisions, and understand how those views were shaped.

Dr. Urie Bronfenbrenner's ecological system is a tool by which the above data is collected. Dr. Bronfenbrenner's research and writings on human ecological systems are world-renowned and applicable in so many different contexts. The original intention of the Bronfenbrenner ecological model was to understand the dynamics of a child's surroundings and the implications they have on the child's development. Today, this model is widely adopted throughout leadership circles and social scientists around the globe.

Now, as I explain how this model works, hold on tight, because we are going to get a bit "social sciencey" for a minute. I promise this will all come full circle, so hang in there with me.

Microsystem: Just the Basics

Urie Bronfenbrenner's theory was presented as a means to view a child's development as an outcome of the ecological system that surrounded the child as they were raised. In this case, an ecological system starts with the child's immediate environment, or microsystem. In Dr. Bronfenbrenner's book *The Ecology of Human Development*, Bronfenbrenner defines the microsystem as "a pattern of activities, roles, and interpersonal relations experienced by the developing person in a given setting with particular physical and material characteristics."[1] What this boils down to is the very basics of a child's surroundings. This initial ecological puzzle piece consists of the child's home, school, immediate family, neighborhood, pets, etc., and is the first layer of their ecological system. There is no connection between these elements at this layer—these things simply exist in the child's world. However, each of these elements has a direct impact on their development. For example, if a child grows up in a home owned by the parents, studies show that there is a direct correlation to higher cognitive test scores. Cognitively, the child doesn't understand this connection, but this part of their ecosystem is directly impacting their development.

> Does homeownership affect the outcomes of resident children? Using a national data set, we observed that children of homeowners have better home environments, high cognitive test scores, and fewer behavior problems than children of renters. We find that these results hold even after controlling for a large number of economic, social, and demographic variables. Owning a home compared with renting leads to 13 to 23 percent higher-quality home environment, ceteris paribus. The independent impact of homeownership combined with its positive impact on the home environment results in the children of owners achieving math scores up to nine percent higher, reading scores up to seven percent higher, and reductions in children's behavior problems of up to three percent.[2]

Mesosystem: Making the Connection

As we zoom out from the microsystem, we move into the mesosystem, which is the child's connections to their immediate environment. A mesosystem is created when two or more elements of a microsystem interact. Bronfenbrenner defines the mesosystem as "a set of interrelations between two or more settings in which the developing person becomes an active participant."[3] As different pieces of a child's microsystem begin to become aware of one another, a mesosystem is born.

The child begins to understand that their family is connected to the neighborhood and that their pets are connected to their home because they live there too. Here is where the child begins to understand their place in their microsystem and mesosystem and how to interact with their surroundings. Bronfenbrenner breaks down this interaction into four categories or types"

Multi-setting participation: Multi-setting participation is the most basic form of social participation. Here, the person interacts in two separate microsystemic social settings. For example, when a child grows into the school age years, their microsystem expands into the mesosystem due to the now increased social setting in which they are interacting—at home and now in a classroom.

Indirect linkage: Indirect linkages are interactions that may involve a third party but will have a direct impact on the individual interaction. An example of an indirect linkage would be the relationship a parent has with a baseball coach. If that relationship is healthy and mutual, that relationship will have a direct impact on the child's personal interactions with that coach. If the parents are actively engaged with the coach and the sport, the parent may spend more time with the child on their pitching or hitting technique. If these two microsystems never interact, morphing into the child's mesosystem, the child could miss out on some amazing growth opportunities, even making it to the big leagues. I know, that was a bit dramatic, but as a former college baseball player, I *feel* the disconnect!

Intersetting communication: Intersetting communication consists of messages sent from one setting to another with the intent of providing specific information to persons in the other setting. Wow, okay, so keeping with the baseball theme for a second, an example of intersetting communication would be a teacher relaying information about a player's grades in a particular class, let's say algebra, to the coach. For me, this was in the form of a phone call from my teacher to the coach, then to my parents, letting them *all* know that if I didn't dramatically change my academic performance, I would no longer be able to play baseball. In this instance, I happily obliged.

Intersetting knowledge: Intersetting *knowledge* is information or experiences that exist in one setting about another. Intersetting knowledge is gained through intersetting communication or from other sources outside the internal setting. Keeping with the theme of my high school baseball career, I am now under fire for slacking off in my science class. I'm picking up a bit of a trend about my high school self. Tying in the example of intersetting knowledge, I decide to write my final science paper on the dynamics and science of a curveball. So I head off to the library and begin combing through physics book after physics book, learning as much as I can on how a ball thrown on a certain plane, at a certain velocity, with a certain spin, can seemingly curve through the air. The knowledge gained through this process not only impacts my interaction in the classroom but also increases my knowledge of a curveball and decreases my Earned Run Average (ERA) by a full point.

Exosystem: External Influences

As a child begins to understand their mesosystem, their aperture widens, and they begin to comprehend their exosystem. Now, the exosystem isn't the ghostly slime projected from unruly ghosts in the 1984 film *Ghostbusters*. That's ectoplasm, and there's a difference. I think I just dated myself. Anyway, a child's exosystem refers to the external settings in the child's environment that impact their development indirectly. Bronfenbrenner speaks of the exosystem as "consisting of one or more settings that do not involve the developing person as an active participant but in which events occur that affect, or are affected by, what happens in that setting."[4] Some examples of a child's exosystem are their parent's friends, extended family, and even colleagues at a parent's workplace. If a parent is promoted at work and receives a raise, this indirectly impacts a child's world, especially at Christmas time.

Let me take you to the bottom of the ninth inning of a championship baseball game. My team is down by one run, there are two outs, the bases are loaded, and I'm at the plate. The runners on each of the bases all had individual experiences at the plate that led to them being on base. Two of them were walked, and the other smashed a hard ground ball to the shortstop, where he was able to beat the throw to first after a small error.

Each of those external interactions, the decisions made by the previous hitters, impact my decision making at the plate. I can tell that the opposing pitcher is feeling the pressure after the error by the shortstop and the previous walks. These are all things that play an important role in my exosystem at the plate. Do I let a few pitches go by and see if he really has lost control of his fastball? Do I swing at the first pitch I can hit? Do I bunt the ball and try to beat the throw to first? All of these decisions and outcomes are possible because of the actions of the previous three hitters. Now, with the game on the line, I have to act based on the present situation. All of these external interactions in this scenario make up my exosystem.

Macrosystem: The Big Picture

To close out the story, I smashed the ball into left field, and we won the game—at least that's how I remember it. Bringing it back to the ecological model, as a child begins to understand their exosystem and how it impacts them, exposure to their macrosystem begins to emerge. Macro, by definition, is something on a larger scale—a zoomed-out view of what shapes our reality. According to Bronfenbrenner's model, the macrosystem refers to indirect influences of a child's life, extending even further out than the exosystem. Examples of a macrosystem would be the ethnic culture in which a child lives, a government or political system by which a child is surrounded, and the child's socioeconomic positionality. The macrosystem, according to Bronfenbrenner, refers to the preexisting culture and situation a child is born into and looks at how that environment affects the child's growth and development.[5]

Chronosystem: That's Life

Finally, the chronosystem. The chronosystem is a correlation of life events, physical transitions, and sociohistorical events that shape a child's worldview. Examples can include anything from moving to a new town, handling a parent's divorce, or having a military parent who is often absent. Chronosystemic events can have a dramatic impact on a child's development. I think we can all recall some critical life events that shaped some part of our operating system.

Moving away from baseball for a minute, for me, my mother's death in 2020 had a profound impact on many different areas of my life. My decision-making calculus and my worldview are different than they were in 2019—in some good ways and in some negative ways. The point is that life events shape our development, even later in life.

*

To summarize Bronfenbrenner's ecological theory and to bring it back into the realm of leadership, everything from the pets we grew up with as kids, to the divorce of our parents, to the car accident we were in last week has an impact on how we view the world around us and how our brains have developed over time. As a leader, understanding some of the foundational pieces and significant events that have occurred in your team members' lives can go a long way in understanding how they operate as employees and what they need to thrive in remote and hybrid work environments.

Now, let's break this down practically. The following story is a true one and represents a dear friend of mine and a recent employee experience he had as a leader of a large company. Names were changed to protect the identity of those involved, but the information is as relevant to Bronfenbrenner's ecological systems theory as it comes. Suspend reality for a minute and put yourself back in Traci's shoes.

Traci has just hired Matthew to join her team, which has recently moved to a hybrid working environment. Throughout the interview process, she found out how Matthew responds to interview questions, because she hired him based on those responses and his résumé. Traci knows Matthew is sharp, quick on his feet, and presents himself well (online at least), but now she wants to know who he is as an individual and what makes him who he is. The only real thing Traci was able to deduce during the hiring process, outside the résumé and interview, is that Matthew was working from a home office. She could hear the kids in the background, his virtual backdrop is one of a vast mountain range that he may or may not have hiked—a clear and all-too-familiar occurrence when your actual background may have a treadmill and a small table with fourteen coffee cups on it.

In order to keep her work environment equitable, Traci has let her team choose their work location, and Matthew has chosen to work mostly from home. Traci is really excited to have Matthew on her team, but he is the first employee ever to be virtually onboarded into the company. Not only that, but Traci will have to begin the process of establishing trust and building a relationship with him mostly through a computer screen and a cell phone. As she searches the internet for tools to help her do this, she finds that some of her colleagues have found success in their use of the Bronfenbrenner ecological model, and she is curious as to its usefulness for this specific case, so Traci decides to give it a shot. As his new boss, she takes the time to study up on the model, jumps on a call with Matthew, explains the Bronfenbrenner model and each of the ecological systems to him, emails him a blank form with six overlapping circles, and asks him to take the day to fill it out. The next morning she is thrilled to open her inbox and find an email with Matthew's responses. Let's take a look at what he has filled out and what it says about him.

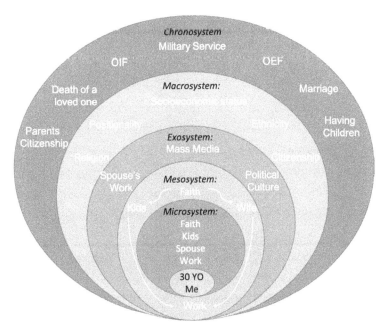

I know . . . it's a beautifully confusing glob of overlapping circles, but the simplicity of this model compared to what a leader can learn from it is pretty astounding. According to Matthew's file, he is a thirty-year-old male who served in the Marine Corps and has an exceptional work history. He's never been fired, has an impressive stack of recommendations, and has more degrees than a thermometer. On paper, he is the perfect candidate to be able to get this job done. But what about Matthew as a person? How do you go beyond a résumé and an interview to really get to know a person? What does this information tell Traci about how he makes decisions?

The use of the Bronfenbrenner model gives us a behind-the-scenes snapshot into what has shaped Matthew's decision-making, his worldview, and ultimately how he wants or needs to be led. Let's start with Matthew's microsystem and work our way outward. What we can tell, right off the bat, is that Matthew is married, has children, some flavor of faith, and believes work is important.

In the most basic terms Matthew's microsystem consists of his faith, his spouse, his children, and his work. These are the foundational reasons behind Matthew's decision making. I realize that these microsystemic elements (please don't tell his wife and kids that I called them "microsystemic elements") seem foundational and straightforward—but that's the point. In the simplest of terms, when making decisions, Matthew thinks about how that decision will affect the elements of his microsystem, as they are the most essential elements of Matthew's life.

As his microsystem elements begin to interact and morph into his mesosystem, thought processes beyond what's essential to him as an individual begin to emerge that identify a much larger picture. Decisions about his work will undoubtedly affect his spouse, children, and potentially his faith. Given that these are foundationally important elements of his life, he will make decisions that will produce the best outcome for his collective microsystem; therefore, his mesosystem drives how he leads, wants to be led, and how he makes important decisions.

As Matthew's leader, looking at his life through the lens of the Bronfenbrenner model, Traci can begin to ask questions about his career aspirations, faith-based activities (if it's appropriate and legal and if trust has been established), and his family because he's already told her that these are important elements of his life. This also tells Traci that he has taken the time to emphasize family in this stage of the model. Listing his family as a foundationally important mesosystem element tells

Traci that Matthew values time with his family and that a good work-life balance is probably important to him. Furthermore, on a fundamental level, it tells Traci that his family is important to him and gives her the opportunity to ask about them and get to know him on a more personal level.

Looking at his exosystem, we find external elements of his life that directly impact and shape him as a person. In this day and age, information overload and media coverage are continuous, and the absorption of information is often subliminal. Things we see on the news, on social media, at conferences, and via the thousand other sources of external information we receive all day long have a tangible impact on human development and our thought processes.

An interesting element of Matthew's exosystem is how his spouse's career indirectly impacts his decision making. This tells Traci that his wife works and that what she does is important to him. I'm going to take some analytic license here for a minute and put myself in Matthew's shoes to break this down practically. If my wife has a great day at work, that can translate to a great day at home together and overflow into the following workday. If my wife gets a promotion and I can stay at home and eat cupcakes all day, the fact that she is an incredibly hard worker and good at her job, neither of which I have control of, still benefits me a great deal. Now, it may not help her as much, but that's not the focus.

The point here is that external factors that may be out of our control, like politics, media, and a spouse's job, have both indirect and direct impacts on our decision making and how we view the world. As Matthew's new boss, not only does this scenario give Traci a talking point for their next meeting; it gives them potential common ground to begin establishing a trusting relationship.

Matthew's macrosystem consists of things that are "in the background" of his decision making. These are elements of Matthew's life into which he was born. Again, these are conversation starters and not meant to be analyzed without conversation. With the information we already know, Traci can begin to ask questions about the macrosystem elements he mentions. As Traci asks about Matthew's macrosystem, specifically his ethnicity and citizenship, she finds out that Matthew is a first-generation American citizen whose family moved to the United States from Mexico only a few months before he was born.

Matthew tells Traci about growing up in a multigenerational household, and that at any given time he could sit down with his grandfather and ask as many questions as he wanted. He unpacks, in detail, scenes of watching his father work long hours with joy in his heart, coming home to a full house and a full dinner table and ending every night with a full heart. He explains that being born into a situation where he had immediate access to his large family was critically important to him growing up, and that he will make career decisions that will make this same experience possible for his children. Now we're getting to the good stuff!

After Matthew explains the details of his macrosystem, Traci begins to peel back the rest of the onion. First, a word of caution when you enter this space as a leader. This area can be extremely personal and uncomfortable to work through. In fact, you may not get into this part of the ecological model until firm trust has been established. This could take months or years or it could never happen, depending on the participant. Never assume anything based on the information provided. Ask probing and clarifying questions and *always* be willing to accept and respect an "I don't want to talk about that" response.

I suggest that you clearly explain this section of the ecological systems theory, letting the participant know that each section will be unpacked at its own pace, and that these experiential elements directly impact decision making and are not to be used outside a professional (work, not therapy) setting. In this stage, the person filling out the blank template of the model is in control. This model is about getting to know how to lead your people, not how to counsel them through traumatic experiences (unless that's your profession). Now, back to the scenario!

Matthew's chronosystem is fascinating! His file has let you know that he was in the Marine Corps, but his chronosystem elements highlight the fact that he was deployed to Iraq and Afghanistan during Operations Iraqi and Enduring Freedom. Traci carefully begins to ask questions about these elements of his chronosystem through the lens of understanding how he needs to be led and how he makes decisions.

He begins with why he joined the Marine Corps in the first place. At the ripe young age of eighteen, he enlisted right after he graduated from high school. He would have gone to college, but the call to serve was just too strong. He enlisted in 2002, a year after September 11, and eight months after graduating from the Marine Corps Recruit Depot in San Diego, he found himself in an infantry battalion headed for Iraq.

He walks Traci through his training, tells her about the Marines he relied on to survive and the amazing leadership team that guided them through intense bouts of combat, bringing him and his friends home safely. He talks about coming home from Iraq and immediately preparing for Afghanistan. As she listens to his story, she can feel the intensity of the scenario and the passion behind the conversation. Matthew talks about the promotions he received before being deployed to Afghanistan, which came with the responsibility of an eight-Marine team. His intensity grows as he talks about leading his Marines into combat and the pride he felt in successfully bringing his Marines home safe.

This man is a warrior and a leader! As *his* leader, Traci knows that she will have to funnel this intensity into productivity and give him opportunities to excel. Some of the main things she has learned about Matthew throughout this process include that he will make business decisions that will benefit him and his family, he can be trusted in tense environments, and he can be relied upon to lead at the drop of a hat. While he hasn't been in the workforce for long, his stack of recommendations comes from three- and four-star general officers and senior noncommissioned officers who intimately know how he performs under pressure. These are the kinds of things Traci can lean on when figuring out how to manage and lead Matthew virtually.

*

Now, a word of caution when using Bronfenbrenner's ecological model. Trust is paramount throughout the entire process. This isn't a one-time sit-down meeting where you absorb a person's life story in an hour. This is a learning process where the employee has complete control of what they share and when they share it. What this gives you as a leader is a baseline for conversation to follow up on. Think of this as a blueprint to getting to know your people. As you construct this blueprint, you make changes, you add and take items away, and you craft the blueprint based on the information shared by the individual. This blueprint morphs over time as trust increases and your people feel well cared for and individually considered.

In a hybrid work environment, trust is essential to the success of your team—both the leader and the followers. The follower must trust the leader to provide whatever they need to get their job done well. The leader must, in turn, understand what the follower needs and provide that to the best of their ability, while trusting that when the employee is given these items, they will perform well.

With a foundation of trust, a focus on individual consideration, and the use of tools like Bronfenbrenner's ecological model, leading and being led in hybrid and remote work environments can be an experience like no other, where we aren't just making the best of a bad situation, but where we are thriving and innovating like never before. Innovation is a key part of successfully operating and leading in a hybrid work environment. Innovation and creativity are what got us here in the first place. But now, how do we continue to push the innovative envelope and make our world a better place? How do we lead toward the future in an ever-changing technical environment that waits for no one? After we take a look at the Questions to Consider and Transformation Tips below, we'll dive into the innovation process and pick apart how to lead teams toward changing the world.

QUESTIONS TO CONSIDER

1. How can you use Bronfenbrenner's ecological systems model with the people already on your team?

2. Does your team trust you enough to give you vulnerable and accurate answers? Why or why not?

3. Would you be able to take a look at your team and fill out their ecological systems charts for them? How well do you know your team?

4. How can you apply this model to team building?

5. What other benefits can you identify from knowing your people this deeply?

6. How do you make decisions? What does your own ecological system look like?

TRANSFORMATION TIPS

1. Yes, Bronfenbrenner's ecological model is very social
    sciencey. The point of highlighting this model is to drive
    home the importance of knowing how your people make
    decisions. The ecological systems in which your people grew
    up have a major influence on how they operate in the
    workplace and will give you, as a leader of hybrid teams,
    insight into how they operate when they are working from
    home.

    ## TIP:

    Take this model and use it as a guide. You don't have to use
    each system in order or every system in totality. Start out
    with the basics, and as you build up a trusting relationship,
    dive in deeper. I promise that if you understand how
    your people make decisions, organizing workloads and
    priorities for you and your team will become clearer and
    your team will operate within their strengths.

2. Before you throw this out to your people, take the assessment yourself. If you want to be a great leader, you have to be aware of who you are as a leader. Take the assessment and be completely honest.

TIP:

As you take the assessment, be aware of the sensitivity of the assessment. Take inventory of how you are feeling as you dive into the deeper ecological systems of your own life. Would you share this with someone without completely trusting them? Do your answers help identify how you make decisions? Self-awareness throughout this process will give you insight into how your team will feel as they unpack their ecological systems. Once you have completed it and if you feel comfortable sharing the results with your team, do so. This will increase trust and give them an inside look into *your* decision-making process. Sure, all of this can be done remotely, in person, or in a hybrid work environment. However, operating in a hybrid environment requires an increased amount of trust throughout the team. The information revealed from this model will ultimately increase trust within the team and help rehumanize a dehumanized work culture.

FIVE

INNOVATION LEADERSHIP
How to Change the World

I think we can all agree that "innovation" has been one of the most popular terms of the twenty-first century—and rightfully so. When I think of innovation, people like Steve Jobs, Bill Gates, Elon Musk, Sheryl Sandberg, and Whitney Wolfe Herd are top of mind. These disruptively innovative minds have created some of the most amazing tools of the twenty-first century, shaping the entire Western way of life. Electric cars, watch phones, dating applications, and, most importantly for me as a parent, the ability to find a trusted person to keep my children alive while my wife and I aren't home.

I'm going to nerd out here for *just* one second, so once again, please bear with me. While these anomalous ideas and companies have had a huge impact on our world, they are an incredibly small percentage of the innovative stratosphere. Innovation does, and should, happen every day, even among us normal folk. Innovation, by definition, is the "practical implementation of ideas that result in the introduction of new goods or services or improvement in offering goods or services."[1] While the term has mainly been associated with the tech industry, innovation goes well beyond the next best smart device. It dives deep into the fabric of an idea that could become a reality and change the world.

What has emerged from the age of innovation is a relatively new leadership philosophy called "innovation leadership." Not a very innovative title but stick with me. Innovation leadership is a philosophy and technique that combines different leadership styles to influence employees to produce creative ideas, products, and services. This deviates a bit from the traditional leadership philosophy of having to move quickly to maintain relevance or else drown. Innovation, by nature, takes time, is often associated with repeated failure, and forces a leader to understand and admit that they themselves don't have all the answers.

The term *innovation* is described as a fluid process through which ideas change and become more refined through trial and error. The spectrum of innovation is limited only by what teams can think up. Ideas such as an urban garden sprawling across the lower level of a skyscraper, the creation of the newest piece of travel technology, and a new way to parent our children are all examples of innovation at its finest.

Innovation *leadership* is a fluid process through which a leader uses different leadership styles to create an environment conducive to creativity, trial and error, and idea generation. The innovative leader, as we will refer to him or her, must be able to float between leadership styles to lead the innovative *process*es more than *manage* a person or team. Sometimes this can get complicated. The innovative leader must be able to give their people enough freedom to be creative while providing the structure necessary to deliver a product. Kinda sounds like this: "Here you go! Go solve the problem however you want, but have something to show the team by Friday." The innovative leader must be able to corral the team's idea into a mission-focused road map, while at the same time encouraging them to try even if they inevitably fail. There are a ton of different methodologies by which the innovative process can be led. Two of the most widely used are the Agile and Waterfall methods.

The Agile process embraces iteration and fluidity. In Agile, failure is not only accepted but embraced. It's a flexible method allowing the airplane to be built as it flies, as long as the airplane continues toward its final destination. Throughout the Agile process, teams will run "sprints," which are short periods of time given to a development team to finish a specific task. Throughout this given period, there are different milestones and deliverables that must meet specific deadlines; however, if there is a need to go back and reassess something, these deliverables can change as the process unfolds. These sprints help to break the project down into measurable and goal-oriented chunks. The collective result of these sprints will be the delivery of a final product.[2]

The Waterfall method is much more deliberate and defined, with very specific deliverables. Iteration takes a backseat to structure in this method. Having a foundation in requirements and specific outcomes, the Waterfall method follows a relatively strict, step-by-step process through which progress is measured.

First, the project requirements are agreed upon right away. These requirements will determine the flow of the entire project. These can be viewed as micro missions that the team can always rely on when they get off track.

Second, the team creates designs of the intended outcome. For technical innovation, this could be a high-level technical solution or program that lays out the purpose and scope of the project. The design can be viewed as the hammer to drive in the nails of the project. For projects outside the scope of technology, this could be a blueprint or schematic.

Third, the team will work through a series of tests and evaluations of how the design is addressing the problem. Does the technological solution work the way we intended? How does the blueprint need to be adjusted? Will this schematic of the building we created hold up to hurricane force winds?

Finally, and most importantly, the product must be deployed and maintained. Innovating is an amazing process, but it's useless if we can't deliver a product that addresses the problem. Yes, there will be maintenance and changes that our team will have to address but having a tangible product at the end of the Waterfall method, or any innovative method, is critical.[3] Otherwise, you have wasted you and your teams time and negatively impacted your credibility.

Okay, stay with me. We are almost to the fun part where we pick back up with Traci, our amazing Director of IT. Research on innovation has uncovered some amazing themes over the past decade. As we apply these themes to hybrid and remote work environments, I want to highlight a few of these themes that directly impact your team's ability to innovate remotely—namely, the three Ds: diversity, driving toward outcomes, and delivery. So, without further pomp and circumstance, let's dive back into Traci's story.

Opportunity of a Lifetime

Now that Traci's team is on a successful path in a hybrid environment, let's see how she leads the innovation process in an industry flooded with good ideas and find out how she gets ahead of the market. As we unpack each of the identified innovation themes, try to put yourself in Traci's shoes. Each of these concepts translates well to in-person and remote teams, so pick apart these concepts and make them yours.

Traci walks upstairs to her newly crafted home office, looks admiringly at her new plants that desperately need water, logs on, and finds an email from the CEO of one of her favorite clients.

Traci! It's a good day here in Southern California! I hope you and your team are settling into this new crazy work life. Seeing what you guys have done with this global transition has been amazing, and I've been able to learn so much from being a part of your transformational coalition. We can talk about that over coffee someday.

I'm writing you this email with a huge smile on my face and with some crazy expectations. Our company, Titanium Consulting, just received a huge contract from one of the largest technical companies on the planet asking us to do something impossible. We've been given a problem to solve, and a timeline, but WE NEED YOUR HELP! Will you and your team combine your superpowers with ours to deliver this thing?

Traci sits back in her chair, eyes as wide as they've ever been, and assesses the situation. The project, the development of a new technology, is right up her team's alley. If this is done right and on time, not only will it be a huge payday for her team, but it will change the lives of millions of people. The first thing on her mind is presenting the opportunity to her team and getting their opinions on the project. She knows that they can do it, but do they? After taking a few deep breaths and thinking through the situation, she starts crafting her email to the team.

Team,

We have an opportunity to help change the way people use cell phones! Our partners at Titanium Consulting have just been awarded a contract to do the impossible. We need to help them create a cellular phone cover that is not only affordable and able to fit most cellular phones, but it has to be solar powered. That's right, we are eliminating the need for cell phone chargers! This will revolutionize the cell phone industry and put us at the forefront of the "next big thing"! If we choose to accept this assignment, we will be working closely with the folks at Titanium Consulting to get this work done. The only guidelines are that the product must be prototyped within six months of us accepting the contract and that we have to prove that it works! That's it! What are your thoughts?

Stepping back for a second, I know solar-powered cell phone covers already exist, but they are *really* cool, so I thought it would be a great scenario to walk through with Traci and her team.

Her team unanimously gives an enthusiastic thumbs-up! Now it's up to Traci to figure out how to organize her team and create a hybrid space to get this work done! She decides to use the Agile method, which will give her team the flexibility to be creative and fluid in their processes. She has a deadline and a problem to solve. Let's walk through her thought process using the themes we identified earlier.

Diversity

Why is diversity important in the innovation process? It's all about diverse ways of thinking. If Traci's team were made up of middle-aged men with engineering backgrounds, there would likely be very little outside-of-the-box thinking. Luckily for her, the team is composed of engineers, leadership experts, project managers, administration gurus, and strong leaders, and it is a multiracial powerhouse. Their ideas are rarely the same, and when organized, their brainstorming sessions have been productive and new ideas have been generated.

Traci starts to strategize. Although the innovation process is wildly creative, Traci knows she has to organize the work and keep the team moving toward outcomes.

How can I use my team's diversity to help solve this problem? I've got ten individuals from different backgrounds, with different skill sets and with different worldviews. All of them bring something different to the table, but how am I going to re-shape them into an innovation machine? Okay, James, Brice, and Braden are my engineering geniuses, but they have moved to different states. I'll structure the weekly requirements and let them create their work schedules.

Traci sets the meeting rotations with herself and her engineers for every Friday afternoon over a virtual happy hour.

This is where her team will show their progress and verbalize their needs, setbacks, and new ideas. Braden has shown some amazing leadership potential, so he will be the engineer who reports the team's findings directly to Traci.

Isabella, Matthew, and Luke are the engineering workhorses on Traci's team. All three of them are recent graduates of some of the best engineering schools in the country. They will take the ideas that James, Brice, and Braden create, and together they will create the prototypes for testing.

The entire project depends on her engineering team's ability to create the impossible. One of Traci's main priorities is to make sure they have what they need when they need it. She needs to create a space where they feel free to report failure and advancements, to dive into crazy ideas and create simple processes, and to get this project done on time and within budget. Her entire team will be organized to support James, Brice, and Braden.

Next, Traci engages her project managers. Shannon and Travis will run the daily operations and manage the project throughout the week. Although they come from extremely different backgrounds and manage projects very differently, their skills complement each other well. Here's Traci's guidance, delivered through a virtual meeting room:

> Guys, I want you both to meet every day and manage this project together. You two are going to be my right-hand people in driving this process toward an actual product that we can present to Titanium Consulting. Shannon, you have a military background, so take what you've learned from the army and motivate

the team. Travis, I need you to use your engineering background to address the technical leadership of this project. Whatever James, Brice, and Braden need, try to make it happen. Other than that, I'm only a phone call away. Check in with me when you need me, and let's drive this thing home!

The administration of this project is going to be a bit tricky. Through her administration gurus, who are also separated by time zones, she will make sure that patents, legal challenges, overtime and PTO approvals, and anything else falling into the "daily logistics" category are handled by Michael and Sarah. Sarah, a lawyer living in Texas, is a deep well of knowledge when it comes to everything considering patents and contracts. Traci calls her to let her know her roles and responsibilities: "Sarah, I need you to make sure the red tape and legal constraints don't get in the way of progress. We need to drive production and let the engineers do their thing." Sarah gives Traci an enthusiastic salute and logs off.

Her next call is to Michael. "Mike! Man, I need you to handle all the administrative actions for the team while we drive this project. We have to keep within company policy regarding PTO and overtime, but I'm empowering you with those decisions and with approval authority. If one of our engineers needs to purchase something, as long as it's within the purview and budget of *this* project, let's make it happen."

And finally, there's the boss lady herself, Traci. Traci will organize the Agile sprints, team schedules, and due outs, drive the team toward the end zone, and create a space that brings her team together—even though they are spread out across the country—to innovate and change the cell phone world. It's her job to report back to Titanium Consulting. Success or failure of the project will ultimately fall on her amazingly well-equipped shoulders.

Diversity takes on so many meanings. Ethnic diversity within a team breeds diverse thought processes, outside-the-box thinking, and ideas that never would have been created without such diversity. Throw in professional diversity, where people's skill sets are different yet complementary, and you've got a recipe for innovation and progress. Traci's diverse team, both ethnically and professionally, has the tools they need to execute. They just need Traci's leadership to pull them all together toward mission accomplishment.

This all seems extremely well organized and simple, correct? Ha! Leadership is never that straightforward. Let's look into the leadership challenges she will and could run into along the way. The next theme we will dive into is driving toward outcomes.

Driving toward Outcomes

What good is amazing innovation if nothing is produced? It's not. With so much on the line, Traci has to be the one to drive her engineers toward the final product. Her engineering team will run into roadblocks. They will get frustrated and feel like they can't finish. At this point, it's up to Traci to dig into her transformational leadership bag and pull out some of that "inspirational motivation" we talked about earlier.

She knows her engineering team. At this point, she knows what makes them tick and how to pull them back from negative self-talk, self-doubt, and the temptation to quit. By continuing to remind them of why they became engineers in the first place and how important they are to accomplishing this goal, she drives them toward the outcome. She gives them the best environment to succeed and the motivation to do so. It doesn't mean that they will—but it means that they will be in the best possible space to do so.

Now the engineers are working with purpose, the rest of the team is cultivating the environment they need to work well, and Traci is making sure it all happens and is reporting up. After five months and twenty-seven days—the amount of time the client has given them—her team has done it. After hundreds of pots of coffee and a few devastating failures, they have a working prototype and are ready to present to Titanium Consulting. Now it's time to deliver!

Delivery

Delivery is not just about delivering the product but about how the product is delivered. Traci knows that without her amazing team, she might be back in Hank's office, unappreciated and underutilized, just waiting on the clock to reach quitting time. But now she has built a hybrid team that has created something so outside the box that we may never have to worry about losing a cell phone cord again. Wouldn't that be nice!

So now it's up to her to deliver the final product *with* her team. The engineering team has provided the heavy lifting for the project, but the rest of the team kept the boat sailing in the right direction the entire time—and all while working remotely. As brilliant as Traci is, her team knows more about the details of the project than she could communicate. Could she put together a great presentation, take a final bow, and walk out of the room with her hands in the air? Absolutely. Is that the kind of leader she is? Absolutely not. So with her entire team together, live and in person for the first time in a year, they head to the Titanium Consulting headquarters in sunny California.

As they land, the fresh, salty air refreshes their senses and gives them an overwhelming sense of relaxation. Over the last six months, the team has worked hard putting in long, oftentimes stressful hours, running Agile sprint after sprint, with necks sore from the whiplash of success and failure, but they did it. They can all feel that overwhelming sense of having created something great.

Their schedule isn't packed, but they still have to use their time wisely. This presentation could launch their team into the innovative stratosphere—but they still have to deliver. The team heads to the hotel to strategize, eat a good meal, and get a solid night's sleep. The meeting is at nine the next morning, and they are pumped!

Traci and her team arrive an hour early, set up and retest the prototype, and prepare for the Titanium team to arrive. As the Titanium team walks in, their CEO greets Traci with a hug and the ever-so-famous head nod and smile to the rest of the team. The room is arranged like so many corporate boardrooms: a few nice leather chairs at the main table with a row of uncomfortable ones along the wall. Traci, being the leader she is, places her team at the table while she takes a literal backseat! After a few seconds of musical chairs, the meeting begins.

After about three hours of presentation and demonstration, sports coats and ties are long gone, and any sense of hierarchy has vanished. Traci's team members have taken turns answering every question the Titanium team could throw at them. "How did you get this done so fast?" "How did you organize the work?" "How should we present this to our customer?" Besides the opening remarks and introductions, Traci only answered one question: "What should we have for lunch?"

Traci empowered every single member of her team with tasks that matched their skill sets and passions. Traci didn't need to answer the engineering questions—she had engineers to do that. Questions about how the project was managed? Those were for Shannon and Travis. Traci led the innovative process through empowerment, and the outcome was a product that could change the world!

*

As you we dive into the Questions to Consider and Transformation Tips below, analyze Traci's innovation story a bit. This process isn't only successful in the innovation world. Traci understands how her team operates and lets them do their work. She drives them toward success by leading them individually toward a specific team goal. She demonstrates her ability to delegate, keep people on task, and recognize and organize several different skill sets

Now a bit of a disclaimer: this is a story about a team that works extremely well in a hybrid environment. It may seem like Traci has the ideal situation and that she doesn't have to really lead anything. But this couldn't be further from the truth. Does Traci exude power and influence? Absolutely. Does she need to lead from a place of authority and hierarchy sometimes? Yes. The secret sauce is how she does that. Let's continue to peel back the leadership onion and look into how Traci uses power and influence, which are both absolutely necessary in a hybrid or remote work environment.

<u>QUESTIONS TO CONSIDER</u>

1. Take a good look at some of the tasks that you have as a
    team. Are your people aligned according to their strengths?

2. How are you engaging your remote or hybrid team and
    motivating them to complete daily tasks or to innovate?

3. Where is there room for innovation in your work with your
    team?

4. Innovation isn't all about technology. In what ways can you
    innovate in your leadership as you lead your hybrid and
    remote team?

5. How well do you trust your people, and how can you increase trust between you and your team members?

6. Are there critical missions or tasks within your organization or team that could be done differently?

TRANSFORMATION TIPS

1. Okay, so, innovation. Again, this isn't always a techy thing. It is often just figuring out how to do something more efficiently than it's currently being done.

TIP:

Take a look at some of your old systems and processes. Dissect how they are accomplished and try to find more efficiency. Also, take a look at your team structure. Are you pulling out and using the best qualities and skills of your team? Continue to ask your team how they are doing and if what they are doing is still stimulating enough to continue doing. In a hybrid world, this will make your team feel like they are part of a much larger vision and mission and will help them identify their true strengths.

2. The innovation process can be amazingly rewarding; however, burnout can happen quickly. Burnout isn't only a concept relating to hybrid teams, but when a team is spread out across neighborhoods, cities, time zones, states, and maybe even countries, your team members may work themselves into the ground without virtual intervention from their leadership.

TIP:

Whether working through the process of innovation or even just delivering a product, check in with each member of your team to gauge how they are doing. When you meet with them, if it's over a videoconference, make sure they have their camera on. This is important in a few ways. 1) You can see their face. Often times you can tell a lot about a person's mental well-being from the look on their face. 2) You are able to see their surroundings and take visual inventory of what they might need. It's also very important to ask the right questions. If you feel like someone on your team is burning out, ask questions about what they are doing to take care of themselves mentally, physically, and emotionally outside the project at hand, and always make sure they know that you actually care about their well-being.

SIX

POWER AND INFLUENCE THEORY
Using Your Powers for Good

Spiderman's late Uncle Ben once said, "With great power comes great responsibility." Spiderman, who has superhuman strength and senses and who can swing across the metropolis from the spiderwebs he shoots from his wrists, has a great amount of influence and power. Eventually, he finds Uncle Ben's killer and corners him. The ethical chess match that ensues within Spiderman's head is intense. Imagine epic superhero music playing in the background . . . *Does Peter Parker take the revenge he's longed for since the death of his uncle? Or does he hand him over to the police in a righteous act of justice? Bum, bum, buuuum!* You get the point.

Leadership naturally comes with power and influence. As a leader, you have the power to make decisions on behalf of your team, you have influence over the decisions made by your organization, and whether you believe it or not, you are a role model for others in the company. Just like Spiderman, you get to choose how we use your power and influence, and if you use it well, you will find that your networks will grow, your teams will succeed, and you will put yourself in a position to increase your power and influence in other areas of work. If you abuse it, you will find yourself alone and potentially out of a job.

While often used interchangeably, power and influence are separate pieces of the leadership puzzle. Power, when we view it through the lens of leadership, can be described as a person's ability to impose their will on someone or a situation. Some schools of thought believe that power is backed up by a title or position, while others see power as a distinctive character trait that can be cultivated through experience and training. Both are correct and are often used together.

Influence is a bit different in that you can have influence while not being in a position of power. Yes, powerful leaders often have an innate ability to influence others, but influence can exist without power, and vice versa.

What we have to do as leaders is take a step back and look at how we use these concepts. In a remote work environment, an employee can't walk by a large corner office, see the "Vice President" sign on the door, and interact with that person on a daily basis. When leading a remote team, the scales tip in favor of influence over power. Now, I'm not saying that power doesn't enter the equation; I'm saying that, as we lead remote or hybrid teams, exuding influence can give you more credibility than exuding power. Let's pick back up with Traci and her team and see how she effectively exudes power and influence.

Traci and her team have returned to their homes and are still beaming from their win in California. They have set a new standard of work, which is great. However, with great success comes great expectation. After a few days of well-deserved PTO, she logs in to find several congratulatory emails in her inbox from the C-level folks at her company.

Traci,

I just received a phone call from the CEO of Titanium Consulting, and he was absolutely raving about you and your team. The work you guys did over the past six months is truly remarkable, and I can't wait for you to debrief me on the entire project. Your performance over the past two years, not only on this project but in helping our organization transform into a hybrid machine, has been impressive. Let me know when you get back in town; I want to run a few things by you. Let's set up a time for us to meet at the office to talk about some of the conversations we've been having as an executive team. Just so we don't keep you in suspense in the meantime, the Bottom Line Up Front (BLUF) is that the executive team wants to move the entire innovation department under your leadership and make you the Chief Information Officer (CIO) of the company. We can talk more about it when we meet. Lunch is definitely on me!

Regards,
Greg
Chief Executive Officer

Needless to say, Traci is floored by this opportunity. Her mind is spinning with all the things she has been wanting to accomplish with this organization that until now required another layer of leadership to get done. She immediately thinks back to her time with her first CEO, Hank. *My, how times have changed. I have worked so hard to get here, but now it's my turn to do this right.* Traci quickly responds to Greg with an enthusiastic acceptance of the meeting. It's simple, and short.

Hi Greg,

> *Thank you so much for your kind words. I just got back in town and will come into the office in two days if that works for you. I'm really looking forward to discussing the cell phone cover project, how amazing our team did, and to discuss the proposition from the executive team. I am truly humbled that you would consider me for this and am looking forward to the discussion.*

Sincerely,
Traci
Director, Information and Technology

Now that she has had the chance to take a deep breath, collect her thoughts, and come back down to Earth, the next email is to her team. Here is where she communicates influence with just a taste of power!

Team,

> *What an amazing two years this has been! Together we've overcome challenges that could have broken us apart. We failed, succeeded, crashed, and thrived, but we were together through it all. I'm so impressed by each and every one of you. There have*

been some great things that have happened because of our work that I want to share with you in person. I have a big decision to make, and I want your input. Let's meet together at the office in the large conference room tomorrow at noon. I'll bring lunch, so just let me know what you want. This is exciting, and I'm so glad to be a part of this team.

Traci

Traci is giving her team the ultimate compliment. She wants their input on the decision to take the CIO position. This is a huge leadership move in a few different ways. First, when we talk about leaders having influence, Traci is giving her team power and influence by asking for their feedback on the decision. The ultimate decision will be up to her, but by collecting data from her team, she is able to make a more informed decision. Second, she is increasing her influence and credibility with her team by inviting them into the process. She is showing them that their input matters and that she values them. This, in turn, increases her influence with the team and empowers her to make decisions.

The team meets the next day, and Traci lays out all her cards on the table. "Guys, the executive team wants to move the innovation team under the office of IT, and they want me to be the new CIO. Before I give Greg my answer, I want to hear from you. What are your thoughts?" Without missing a beat, her team slowly stands up and begins a sarcastic slow clap. "Traci! This is what you've been working toward your whole life! We couldn't be happier for you!" Having led the team from its inception, she has built up a level of trust that cannot be rivaled by any title or power position. Her team loves her and would follow her anywhere.

The next day, Traci walks into the same boardroom to meet with Greg, and just as she thought, he was sitting there with a printed-out job offer for the CIO position (he's a great leader but a bit old-school). Greg begins his pitch:

> Now, before you sign this, I want you to be aware of a few things. You will no longer be leading your team directly. You will need to promote or hire someone into your old position, and they will be responsible for your team moving forward—with your oversight, of course. Also, the innovation and IT leadership teams will all report directly to you. That's two organizations making up fifty-six total individuals, and you will be responsible for creating a new strategy and new vision for both organizations and for their ultimate success, failure, and leadership. Some of the team members really wanted the CIO position, and you may face some resistance while you're in the seat. You are going to have to show them a great deal of power and be able to convince them that you are the right person for this job. You have my utmost confidence as well as that of my executive team, but that will only take you so far. Do you think you can handle all of that?

Traci looks at Greg, and with a confident and determined "yes," she signs the paperwork and immediately begins to come up with her engagement strategy. Greg says, "Great! We will get the paperwork ready and make the announcement in a webcast next week. We anticipate amazing things from you and this organization, Traci. Always remember, we have your back!" What a great example of another great leader, right?!

Now, Traci is faced with a challenge that most of us would beg for. She is about to be the first female CIO of her company and must, once again, build a team (a much larger team) that can continue to scale, innovate, and thrive in a hybrid work environment! Let's take a quick break from Traci's story and get into the academics behind *how* Traci is going to display her power and influence over this new larger organization for which she will be responsible.

Take a walk with me to the past. Back to the 1950s when hybrid work wasn't yet a thing yet the theoretical concepts of power and influence were divided into different categories by social psychologists John French and Bertram Raven and turned into theory. The categories of Power and Influence Theory (P&I) as described by French and Raven are that we will focus on are Legitimate P&I, Reward P&I, and Expert P&I. Each of these different forms of power and influence make up the overall theory, but let's pick each one apart, dive into what they are, and demonstrate how Traci uses these concepts to lead her hybrid team and organization.[1] We'll walk through each of these and show how Traci does, or does not, use these different elements or power and influence.

Legitimate Power and Influence

The first concept in the P&I theory is the idea of a formal and hierarchical leadership structure. Conceptually, this means that people will listen to you because you have a legitimate position of leadership. This has very little to do with the kind of leader you are, just that you are in a position to lead. Legitimate power is simple. Elected officials or people with what could be considered "esteemed" titles, such as CEO, president, and principal, are all examples of leaders with legitimate power.

Legitimate power works well in military, government, and political structures; however, the legitimacy, for the lack of a better term, of the position is based solely on the ability for a leader to maintain that position. Without the title, there is no leadership. Furthermore, legitimate leadership can also be contingent upon the situation being led. If a general manager of a baseball team tells the head of marketing for the team to start a new advertisement campaign, the head of marketing will likely comply. If the general manager of the team tells a pitcher how to throw a better changeup, the closer is likely to ignore the businessman running the baseball team.

This isn't all bad news! Those with legitimate P&L have a ton of great opportunities to lead well, especially in the corporate and government environment. This kind of leadership provides a sense of credibility right off the bat. When leading a hybrid team, legitimate leadership is not only a huge part of running the day-to-day operations, but it's pivotal in onboarding new virtual employees. Someone jumping on w a brand-new team has to know that they are talking to the right person and that person has the legitimate authority to guide them through the onboarding process and help them overcome obstacles. Legitimate leadership gets dangerous when the leader is only relying on their position or title to influence and exude power. How many times have you heard the phrase, "Because I'm in charge, that's why!"? Not a good look.

Traci's job is to use her new title to begin conversations with her direct reports. She will have to lean on her legitimate leadership title to influence her new team to follow her, but she will only use this to open doors to conversations and insert influence. Foundationally, Traci's leadership style is transformative and inclusive. She wants to show her teams that, while she is the CIO and ultimately responsible for making decisions on behalf of the organization, she will lean heavily on data and input from her team to make decisions. She promises them, "I will do my best never to make decisions in a vacuum. We are a team. Not one of us has all the answers, and our collective brain power is more useful than mine alone, so we are all in this together. I've got your back!"

Reward Power and Influence

Everyone likes to be rewarded for doing a good job. A "good" leader also likes recognizing their people for things they've done well. It's just a good practice. Reward P&I is the idea that a leader has the ability to promote, reward, and extrinsically motivate their people when possible. One pitfall in this is that the one leading or providing promotion opportunities may not have the actual authority or ability to provide these types of rewards.

To dive a bit deeper into the psychology of intrinsic reward, and to pull a bit of information from the first chapter on transformational versus transactional leadership, if you have to rely solely on rewards and extrinsic motivation to lead your people, you probably aren't paying enough attention to the actual individuals being led.

Transactional leadership has its place. Like I said, everyone likes to be rewarded for their hard work. Bonuses, plaques, and trophies give us a tangible sense that we have done well, and these are amazing tools in a leader's toolbox. However, research over the years has shown that employee retention and overall job satisfaction have little to do with how many plaques employees have hanging on their walls. What the research shows is that, when employees are intrinsically motivated, through a leader's knowledge of how they want to be rewarded, how they want to progress in their career, what their life goals are, and why they do what they do, employees feel more included in the culture rather than just part of a company.

However, this is situational. When we tie reward P&I to hybrid work, specifically remote work, transactional leadership becomes increasingly necessary. I'm not saying that you have to give your people bonuses every time they complete a task. What I *am* saying is that, since you and your people are spread out across the country or city, you must be able to connect in some way. Sending out an onboarding gift, presenting a company T-shirt for a job well done, or offering financial incentives are amazing ways to build up a relationship that is largely based on interactions through a computer screen.

Throughout Traci's first year as CIO, she has had face-to-face interactions with each of her direct reports and with most of their direct reports to get their input on the vision and mission of the department. She wants to change the culture of the organization to one of innovation, respect, inclusion, diversity, equity, and integrity. Each quarter, she holds a weeklong innovation challenge where she breaks her organization up into teams. Leaders change titles with project managers, and project managers switch spots with engineers, etc. The point is to mix things up and have fun with it. She initially runs into resistance with the directors of the teams, but through the proper use of her legitimate power and influence, she wins over the crowd.

Each of the teams is given the ability to pick their own project as long as it is an innovative solution to a business problem that they've identified. It has to be directly tied to the vision and mission of the company. They are given a small budget and told to get moving! Those are the only rules. At the end of the challenge, the entire organization is invited to a dinner where they are wined and dined, and a winner is declared. The winning team not only gets rewarded with a fancy plaque, but their idea or solution will become an active program within the organization. This would come with a specific budget and resources to push the limits of their idea and create something new for the company.

This is an example of combining both intrinsic and extrinsic rewards. Traci knows what drives her teams intrinsically, while at the same time, it gives them an extrinsic reward to fulfill the part of their brain that loves physical recognition. I understand this is a very specific case example, but I want you to analyze it and put it to use in your organization. There are a few things you need to do in order to pull this off. First, you have to know your people. What drives them to succeed? Is it money, recognition, or the chance to create something of their own? How can you use this information to create a plan for both intrinsic and extrinsic motivation and reward your people and teams accordingly?

Expert Power and Influence

Expert P&I is about using your expertise as a leader. We all have a certain amount of expertise in a specific field or practice. After decades of trying new things, I have overwhelming expertise in failure and recovery. In every one of my failures, I've been able to learn something new and recover from failure more quickly each time. The premise behind expert P&I is that if you have a deep level of experience, knowledge, or education surrounding a certain topic, you have likely had success in that field. With this success comes credibility. With credibility comes influence. It's a simple yet powerful concept that basically says that if you know what you're talking about it and can back it up, people will listen to you and follow you.

Some of the pitfalls of being an expert leader is that we can put blinders on, actively ignoring other points of view and expertise. Since *we* are the subject matter experts in our fields, if we aren't careful, we can ground ourselves in the facts that *we* know or *believe* to be true and miss out on opportunities to grow, learn, and make some really great friends.

Way back in chapter 1 we learned that Traci graduated summa cum laude with an undergraduate degree in computer science and engineering, finished up her MBA, has worked her way up to become the CIO of her company, and has overcome professional obstacles that have sharpened her skills as a leader and as a person. She has the *expertise* necessary to take this CIO position and the organization she leads in one of two ways (there are probably more, but let's focus on the big picture).

The first scenario is that Traci runs the organization in a way that is exclusive of her so-called subordinates' input. She could say, "I'm the expert. I have been with this company for fifteen years and have created some of the most game-changing policies and products the world has ever seen!" Traci has earned her legitimate place of power and influence, no doubt, but does that really sound like the kind of leader she is?

The second and more likely scenario is that she uses her expertise to lead rather than dictate. As she walks *with* her direct reports on the innovation process, individually considering her employees and driving success through inspirational motivation, she is creating a legacy that will long outlive her time with the company (we'll talk about that next). Yes, she has worked hard her entire work life to get to where she is, but instead of seeing this as the peak of her career and her time to be in charge, she uses her expertise to create an organization that will change the world—not to become a CIO that will change the world.

Traci knows that her engineers are in a better place to engineer the products and that her human resources specialists are probably better equipped to manage the HR issues that come up than she would be. Could she handle them? Yes! Would it likely be quicker, smoother, and overall better if she let the experts take care of it? Probably! What she does know is that she has a keen ability to inspire and influence her people through personal interaction with a layer of Legitimate P&I that inherently comes with the CIO title.

What Traci does with her power and influence is empower and influence her people to be better. She could very well use her power and influence for evil or corrupt purposes, but she chooses to use what she has earned to create an environment where her people feel included, supported, empowered, seen, and heard. In a hybrid work environment, Traci understands that personal interaction, whether it's through corrective action or reward, is even more important when you are engaging with your people over a computer screen, once a week in the office, or over the phone. What Traci is building is an organizational culture that will outlast her time as CIO. She's building a legacy of inclusion and empowerment. Let's round out her story and see how she solidifies the legacy. Not the legacy of "Traci" but a cultural legacy that will remain long after Traci retires to the beach.

QUESTIONS TO CONSIDER

1. How do you use your power and influence to get a job done?

2. What would your employees say about how you exude power and influence?

3. How do your peers and those above you use power and influence?

4. How can you mix intrinsic and extrinsic rewards based on your team's or organization's needs and wants?

5. Take a look at your expertise. How can the people on
   your team contribute to your knowledge base or teach you
   something?

6. How can you use your legitimate power and influence to
   start conversations and provide "top cover" for your teams?

TRANSFORMATION TIPS

1. Power and influence are amazing tools of leadership. They can be used to break into areas of business never before breached and to maintain positions of influence that are used to change the world.

TIP:

There are other elements of Power and Influence Theory: referent P&I (using your ability to be liked to influence), coercive P&I (forcing people to do what you want based on your position), and informational P&I (controlling information and who receives this information to control people's knowledge base). A summary of Power and Influence Theory is that these six categories highlight how we can use our power and influence for good or for evil. As a leader, you have power and influence. It came with the job. As you dissect these P&I categories, tailor them to how you would want your boss to use them with you.

---

2. I want to give you an answer to a question I get often. How do you regain power and influence once it's gone or changed?

TIP:

Positions change. Leadership and organizational changes often come with company reorganization and transformation. With the switch to hybrid work, this has become common. If you find yourself in a position where you have a decreased level of power, you are in a great place to increase your ability to influence in a positive way. One of the greatest things a leader who has been moved to a perceived decreased power position can do is "adapt and overcome." That phrase was drilled into our heads in the Marine Corps, and it has been a foundational component of my life. Power may shift, but you are a person of influence who can help others succeed.

SEVEN

LEAVING A LEGACY
Your Footprints in the Cultural Sand

All right, so far we've walked alongside Traci from her time as Hank's administrative assistant to her new role as Chief Information Officer of a major technology company. We've witnessed the transformation of her organization as she morphed it into a hybrid giant, leading with integrity, empowerment, and authority. She's created an organization that is set up to succeed, but how does she ensure that the culture she has built is maintained after she is gone? What will the cultural legacy of her organization look like, and how can she influence that in a hybrid work world?

Legacy, in this context, can be defined as the impact someone makes within an organization where the culture they've built not only survives but thrives well beyond their tenure. Personally, when I think of someone who built a legacy to be proud of, I think of Dr. Martin Luther King Jr. Dr. King's impact on our way of life will be felt for generations to come. Talk about a servant and transformational leader. Dr. King's ability to display humility, humanity, and love while simultaneously exuding strength and authority changed the way we view the world.

While we could go on for pages about the impact of Dr. King's life, one example of his legacy was the march on the Alabama state capitol in 1965. Dr. King led thousands of nonviolent demonstrators to the steps of the capitol in Montgomery, Alabama, to increase the number of Black registered voters in the county. Along the way, the group faced incredible acts of violence from law enforcement and other activist groups, and as the demonstrators walked, twelve hours a day for five days, their story went viral. As they moved into Montgomery, they found that their movement inspired fifty thousand Black and white supporters who met them at the steps of the capitol building to join them in their demonstration. In a day without social media, compelling fifty thousand people to gather in one place at one time is an act of inspiration in and of itself. The fact that those people gathered in Montgomery because they believed in the cause and the importance of what he was creating is historic. Dr. King's legacy likely surpassed his own expectations and will continue to inspire people for generations to come.[1]

While we couldn't talk about legacy without mentioning Dr. King, another amazing legacy builder, whose work on rehumanizing leadership will be taught for generations, is Dr. John Maxwell. You can't even talk about leadership without mentioning Dr. Maxwell. My favorite quote from Dr. Maxwell is, "We cannot become what we need by remaining what we are." If that doesn't encompass the point of this entire hybrid book, I don't know what does.

Dr. Maxwell's leadership philosophy is that "everything rises and falls on leadership." In other words, success, failure, team cohesion, team morale, and retention all fall on how we lead our people—they are people after all. The legacy that Dr. Maxwell will one day leave behind gives us a road map on to how to become a successful leader of people. Dr. Maxwell's twenty-first law in his best-selling book *The 21 Irrefutable Laws of Leadership* is the law of legacy. The foundational point of this law, stated by Dr. Maxwell, was that a "leader's lasting value is measured by succession."[2] Firmly believing that the true measure of how well you lead is based on how well you've influenced the people who will remain after you're gone, Maxwell uncovers the true meaning behind leadership. In the Marine Corps we had a saying: "Always leave a place better than when you got there." This is a great goal, but true leadership isn't only about leaving a place in a better state than when you got there, but about equipping the next generation of leaders to make it even better.

A third example of a legacy in progress is the former CEO of IT Cosmetics, Jamie Kern Lima. Jamie is a powerhouse for women, a revolutionary change agent, and an amazing leader. Jamie cofounded IT Cosmetics after realizing that the cosmetics she had been using for years as an award-winning television anchor didn't work for her skin type—so she decided to create ones that did. The mission of IT Cosmetics, beyond the actual cosmetics, is to help everyone feel confident through their line. Jamie started the line in her bedroom and eventually sold it to L'Oréal for $1.2 billion. While that is very impressive, that's not what her legacy is about. The legacy she is building isn't just about cosmetics. As a speaker, writer, and women's advocate, she is changing the narrative on what confidence is and what it should look like. She inspires women to be confident in who they are and empowers them to believe in themselves. Her passion for helping other entrepreneurs like herself succeed is changing lives and creating a long-lasting legacy for future generations of women to follow.

Leaving an inspiring legacy is something we should all strive for as leaders. Hopefully, two to three years after we log off for the last time or turn in our office badges, our names are remembered for our excellent treatment of our people, the culture we created, and of course the advancement of the business without compromising the people-first business model. The concept of legacy leadership isn't difficult; however, leaving an inspiring legacy takes an entire career of work. Conceptually, as a leader moves through different levels of leadership, they leave behind trends, traits, and tendencies that are inevitably emulated by their employees. It's almost subconscious. If someone, not necessarily a subordinate, likes how they are being led, they will take what they like from their leader's style and adapt it to their own.

That's the concept. I say that leaving an *inspiring* legacy takes an entire career of work because an inspiring legacy is the outcome of a lot of things done well over a long period of time. I use the term *inspiring* because not all legacies are good ones. If a leader is consistently leading in a way that is counterproductive to building trust, strong working relationships, equitable partnerships, and empowerment, the legacy left behind won't be one that anyone will want to emulate. Hopefully, that kind of legacy will be forgotten and shredded along with the documentation supporting it.

As we pick back up with Traci, we find her eight years into her position as CIO, a long time for someone in her position. After a few years of growing pains, having consolidated the innovation and information technology departments, including several digital and physical transformations that have shaped her organization into a powerfully efficient machine, her organization is thriving in their hybrid work life. New technologies and partnerships are flowing out of the different departments, and they have molded this hybrid work environment into an efficient and enjoyable way of life. They are now meeting every Wednesday and Friday in the office and have strong policies in place for remote work. Yes, they have to have their cameras *on*!

It's been eight years as a CIO, ten years as a director, five years as an engineer, and five as an administrative assistant. Traci is ready for a beach and a poolside waiter. She's worked incredibly hard over the years and has built something to be proud of—a culture of inclusion, empowerment, trust, and success. Over the last year or so, she has been covertly on the lookout for her successor. As she sits in her home office, pondering her future over a strong cup of coffee, she thinks, *This kid Braden . . . There's just something about him. He took over for me after my promotion, and after a few face-plants, he's been able to do some amazing things that would have taken me a lifetime to accomplish. He's a great engineer and leads the team with a sense of urgency I never had. He is innovative, positively disruptive, and has an edge to him that you need in this position. I need to keep my eye on him.*

Braden has been with the company even longer than Traci. He came into the organization straight out of the Massachusetts Institute of Technology with a graduate degree in mechanical engineering. The guy knows his stuff, that's for sure. James, Brice, and Braden have been the A-team of the engineering organization since they worked directly for Traci back in the "solar cell phone case" days.

Once Braden took over as the director of the entire team, his leadership skills really blossomed. One of the main reasons he excelled in leading his team is because he asked Traci great questions. So many times during Traci and Braden's one-on-ones, he would say, "I have this engineering thing down, but I'm earning a leadership PhD by watching you lead this team." A constant learner, Braden became a student of leadership and has crafted his leadership style through trial and error and a bunch of information Traci was happy to give. She made it easy for him to grow and empowered him to fail forward. Braden is just one example of the fruit of Traci's leadership throughout the years.

As Traci starts to go over her finances and plan for her retirement, she starts to consider her options. She is pretty sure Braden is the person for the job, but she has to be sure. So, like she's done so many times before, she gathers her direct team of peers and the CEO of the company into the conference room to announce her retirement, and like any good leader should, she outlines her timeline and plan for succession. "I'm giving you my two-month notice. Within the next month, I want to have my successor named, vetted, and hired. I want to leave the last month for turnover, leaving plenty of time for a smooth transition. After I retire, and after a few months of vacation, I will be available to you all as a consultant until I'm no longer needed—but I'll leave that timeline up to you." Her colleagues and the CEO sadly agree to her terms, knowing that her successor is going to have some huge shoes to fill.

After she talks to her peers, it's time to relay the information to the direct team leads. This meeting goes a little bit differently.

"First, I want to thank you all. Thank you for supporting me, encouraging me, teaching me, and following me as we've changed the world! Together we have made hybrid work not only sustainable but preferred. We've created some of the most amazing technology the world has ever seen, and we've made people's lives better. That's what it's all about. That's why we do this—to make lives better. We have been there for each other through some of the most difficult times and through some of the most amazing times, but now it's time for me to step down and retire." Traci doesn't talk about the financial bottom line. She doesn't talk about how hard she worked to get to where her career has ended. She talks about the relationships she has made and the impact those relationships have had on *her* personal life and the lives of so many others. She closes the meeting with an open forum for her staff to talk about what they want to see in the next CIO.

The search is on! Traci *carefully* crafts the job description to match the data she has collected from her team and her peers. She wants the job description to be free of any personal bias and written in such a way as to draw a diverse pool of candidates. Let's be clear: she knows that Braden is a good fit for this job, but is he the *best* fit?

As the résumés pile in, Traci enlists the help of her peer group (volunteer army) to narrow down the final three candidates who will be interviewed. Each of them will choose one person from the stack and will sit on the interview panel. As she initially sorts through the stack of résumés, she comes across Braden's, and without looking at it, she places it on the pile of one of her colleagues. If he is chosen for an interview, it will be because one of her colleagues, not just she herself, believes he is a good fit.

The panel narrows down the résumés to the final three, and surprise, at the top of the stack is Braden's résumé. Underneath Braden's résumé are two other candidates who on paper seem to be amazing candidates as well. Tim is a current CIO from another company; he would be an outside hire. Traci has been impressed by his work for years, and they have worked together on a few projects. His credentials are by far the best of the bunch. The other résumé is Sarah's. Sarah is the lawyer who was on Traci's team for the Titanium project and is an absolute rock star. With a law degree from Yale, she has the academic pedigree that would be well respected by everyone and the company experience that gives her a bit of an edge. She is a natural born leader with an unrivaled drive for success—and Traci selects her for the interview.

Hybrid work has made the interviewing process a bit different. Since two out of the three candidates are out of state, all the interviews must be over videoconference. Even though Braden is local, interviewing all the candidates in the same way levels the playing field. This is a policy that Traci set into motion early on in her hybrid conversion. Instructions on how to log in for the interview have been sent to each of the candidates three days in advance, and they have all confirmed that they received and understand the instructions.

The first interview is with Tim. His interview is scheduled for nine in the morning, but roughly fifteen minutes before the interview, the panel logs on and talks about how the interview will be conducted. They go over the order of questions and how they will organize follow-up questions based on the candidate's answers. The group is prepared and waiting on the candidate to log in. As 9:00 a.m. comes and goes, a silence begins to overtake the virtual interview room. This immediately sends up red flags across the panel, and they begin to get concerned. *Where is he? Did we send the instructions? Is he waiting in some random waiting room that we don't know about?*

At about 9:05, Traci gets a notification that Tim is waiting in the virtual "lobby." For a split second, she thinks about letting him sit there for a few moments, but then clicks the allow button to bring him into the interview, anticipating an explanation as to why he was late. However, his face pops onto the screen, and he gives no indication that he has done anything that would warrant an explanation. He says, "Good morning. I'm so glad to be here."

Now, I know that five minutes isn't a huge deal. But for Traci, even if she was three minutes late to a team meeting, she would make sure that her people knew that it wasn't her intention to be late, it wasn't her intention to waste her people's time, and it wasn't her intention to make them wait on her. Tim's inability to recognize that his late arrival would have an impact on the rest of the team was an immediate red flag and would ultimately cost him the job. This may not be a big deal to some, but Traci is trying to help carry on the values that have made her successful—and being on time or else explaining why you were late is a big one.

Sarah's interview was scheduled for 10:00 but has to be pushed to 10:15 due to the time shift from Tim's interview starting late. Sarah, who has been logged in since 9:55, is eagerly awaiting her time to shine. Since the interview team have already had their time to talk about the flow of the interview, they start the interview promptly at 10:15, opening with an apology from Traci about their tardiness with the interview. Sarah is more prepared than she has ever been. As a lawyer, she has every piece of evidence available to show that she should be the next CIO.

Equipped with every legal and mathematical statistic known to the tech industry, Sarah answers every technical question perfectly. Her knowledge of the company, the current state of the industry, and of the future of the industry is clear. She knows how to navigate the legal system of the industry better than anyone ever could. Her processes are seamless, and her procedures are well thought out. Questions regarding the future of the business and the industry are answered better than even Traci could, but when it comes to the leadership questions, Sarah's area of weakness begins to show.

Sarah, with all her legal expertise and statistical knowledge of the industry, is lacking in her ability to lead *people*. Sarah is an amazing technical leader and will take this company to new heights, but will she maintain the culture that Traci has worked so hard to build? Will she lead the people in a way that will empower them and instill trust, or will she drive them toward statistical models that will potentially put them in a box? Let's be clear, this is not about Traci's ego. This is about cultivating and growing a culture that has a proven track record of success. Sarah is amazing. But she is not the right person for *this* position.

Now it's Braden's turn. Sarah's interview has gone a little bit over time, pushing his interview from 11:15 to 11:30. Braden's been logged in since 11:25, just in case—Sarah did the same thing. As the group logs in, they notice that Braden is in a nice sports coat and has a pen in hand, ready to take notes. He's not worried about the time shift and warmly greets the panel, though Traci once again apologizes for the delay.

As the interview progresses, Braden's deep knowledge of the current and future state of the industry is impressive. Although he doesn't have Sarah's statistical knowledge, he knows that if he empowers his team to tackle any given problem without fear of failure, he will *create* statistics and not be bound by them. Every answer Braden offers involves the incorporation of his team, emphasizing how, regardless of the challenge, they would undoubtedly get the job done in a way that had never been done before. He knows how to bring the best out in people, push them when they need to be pushed; he knows when he needs to jump in and get his hands dirty; and he leads with integrity and passion.

As the morning ends, the interview panel collects their notes and moves into the conference room to make their decision. Even though they have conducted the interview online, they themselves are all in the office. They weigh strengths and weaknesses, potential, and longevity. They want to make sure they pick the right person. The company is in a state of hyper growth and is doing very well, but a big part of that is the way Traci's organization has been led. Ian, the CEO, jokes, "Well, I guess we can't find anyone, so, Traci, you're just going to have to put that beach house on hold for a few more years." Everybody laughs, except Traci. After carefully weighing the data, they have decided. It's unanimous. Braden will take over for Traci as CIO and carry on the legacy that Traci will leave behind.

Traci is very excited and has the honor of telling Braden in person. The following week, after all the paperwork and vetting is completed, she sends Braden an email asking him to come into the office for a one-on-one. This isn't uncommon. They've had weekly meetings together to discuss their challenges, business needs, and personal needs. This one, however, will be a bit different.

They walk into Traci's office, and she kicks off the meeting, saying, "If there is one thing that is consistent in every professional situation, you will have people who want to move up in leadership and people who don't. The key is to lead them each in a way that makes them feel empowered to meet their goals—whether that's a promotion or the cultivation of a new idea. Not everyone wants to lead, but for those who do, you must lead them in a way that increases their desire to lead and promotes the best attributes of their leadership. It's not about creating a bunch of mini yous. It's about showing them the foundations of good leadership and highlighting the strengths you see in them." That's what Traci does best. "Braden, I am offering you the CIO position, congratulations!"

Throughout her leadership journey, Traci has pulled out the best in her people. She has empowered her engineers to be the best engineers in the business, given her project management team the chance to succeed and taught them the value of failure, and made sure that she individually considered each and every one of her direct reports—even more so when they moved to hybrid work. Furthermore, she has made sure that her leaders were doing the same. Her consistent drumbeat of individual consideration and empowerment have become engrained in the culture she has so carefully created. Yes, she has had to fire people, and people have quit on her over the years. There have been times when she just wanted to turn her camera off and pretend that her internet went out. But that's leadership—it's hard, and sometimes we may want to go back to a time when we were only responsible for ourselves. When done well, the true fruit of your labor will be seen long after you are gone.

After accepting the job, Braden sits down with Traci for their first peer discussion. Braden unfolds a piece of paper from his pocket and begins to read.

Traci, I have had the privilege of being led by you for eighteen years now. You have cared for me when my mother passed away, pushed me when I was being lazy, inspired me when I failed, and empowered me every step of the way. I have learned everything I know about leading people with compassion and individual consideration from watching you. There have been times when we disagreed, argued, and had some really tough conversations, but you always came back to me to make sure that we moved forward in a healthy way. The culture you built will last for as long as I'm CIO because that's the culture people want to be a part of. My hope is that when it's my turn to leave this building, the next person in line will make this place better than I did. And I learned all of that from you.

Traci stands up and with tears in her eyes gives Braden a huge hug. They go over a few things, and with a heavy but extremely full heart, Traci takes her name off the door.

QUESTIONS TO CONSIDER

1. What four words describe the legacy either of the leader you replaced or a leader you admire in your organization?

2. What four words describe the sort of legacy you want to leave behind?

3. How would your peers describe your leadership and the legacy you will leave behind?

4. What would your employees say about how your legacy has impacted them?

5. How has the culture of your workplace changed with remote and/or hybrid work?

6. Are there people you would trust to carry on your legacy? Who are they, and what makes them worthy of your trust?

TRANSFORMATION TIPS

1. Legacy building takes time, but don't worry about messing up.

> ### TIP:
>
> Legacy building can sometimes feel overwhelming. When I mess up as a leader, I immediately think about how I've tarnished the legacy I've been trying to build. I have to quickly snap myself out of this mind-set and understand that I am human. I make mistakes. As a leader, it's also my job to rectify my mistakes and make things right. That's a part of legacy building too. Being able to say that you were wrong and put in the effort to resolve the problem is a difficult but necessary part of leadership.

2. The legacy of your leadership will be realized after you are gone; otherwise, perhaps you've just been managing. Consider the difference between leadership and management.

TIP:

Dr. Maxwell says it so well: "A leader's lasting value is measured by succession." As you walk through your leadership journey, remember to walk, not run. Take the time to understand issues, people, things, businesses, and most importantly, yourself. This may sound a bit vain, but what are your people going to say about you when you leave the room? Will they say that your leadership has changed their lives for the better and created a culture that they want to be a part of, or will they say that, if they were in charge, they would change everything? Foundationally, legacy begins with how you treat your people, how you run the business, and how you handle failure. Nail those three things, and your legacy will be one that outlives your successors.

CONCLUSION

PULLING IT ALL TOGETHER

Wow, thank you! Thank you for sticking with me through this hybrid leadership journey. We covered a lot of ground here, so let's pull it all together. Transformational leadership is really a foundational leadership model for hybrid work. The four tenets (individual consideration, intellectual stimulation, inspirational motivation, and idealized influence) are all grounded in knowing your people. In a hybrid work environment, knowing how to challenge your people, what drives them, and what their concerns are will solidify trust. Just remember that trust is gained slowly and can be lost quickly.

As we moved away from the individual and focused on the organization, Kotter's eight steps guided us through Traci's shift to a hybrid work world. Kotter's eight steps aren't to be used as a strict checklist for organizational change. Instead, look at the steps as a guide for organizational change. The key points include having the right people in your corner and gaining the trust of those being impacted by the change you are trying to create. Adapt, adjust, and mold these steps into your organizational framework, and use the eight steps as a guide.

Whether we are talking about leading individuals, teams, or changing organizations, things will undoubtedly go wrong at one point or another. Contingency leadership is based upon theory, which states that a leader will fall back on their personal leadership style when things go wrong. Like a mountain lion spooked by a hiker, it's very primitive. We default to what feels comfortable and safe. The SMEAC acronym gives you another simple framework after which to model your leadership. Step one, understand the situation (S), or problem, that you are facing. Take your time to think through the problem, and don't rush to conclusions. Step two, fall back on your mission (M). Relying on the mission will help you to focus on what needs to get done and how to do it. The execution (E) phase is where you gather the tools and people you need to get the job done. Align each team member's skill set with a piece of the problem and trust them to do the work. Now that you know what has to be done and who will do it, the administration and logistics (A) phase is where you lay out *how* you are going to get it done. This is the bridge that will take you from crisis to mission accomplishment. Finally, command and control, or communication (C). Your leadership will be tested during times of crisis. The command and control phase of contingency planning relies on you leading the team, stepping in when necessary, and pushing your team to succeed. Sometimes this part of contingency leadership can get messy, but with trust and a common vision, you and your team can overcome any challenge.

After discussing the need for contingency leadership, we moved into Bronfenbrenner's ecological systems model. We took some liberty in adapting this from childhood systems into a tool that can be used to understand why people make decisions. As we break down an individual's ecological systems, we can identify strengths, weaknesses, and leadership potential in an individual. This tool is also extremely helpful when assigning tasks. If we understand how a person makes decisions, we can gain a pretty good understanding of how they will solve a problem or attack a project.

Bronfenbrenner's ecological systems model gives us the data we need to understand the innovation process and how to lead it. Innovation leadership is all about aligning skill sets to create something new. The innovation process can be maddening to a leader! No one actually wants to fail. It's counterintuitive to a leader's mind-set. But being able to embrace failure, move forward, and keep your team motivated will give you and your team the opportunity to create something great. Put the right people in the right seats on the bus, and just drive it. Avoid potholes if you can, but when you blow a tire, it's your job to get out and fix it and then keep driving.

Once you've changed the world with your innovative products, your power and influence are bound to increase! How do we use power and influence for good and not evil? Here's a start: use your legitimate title and position to exude influence more than show off your power. Your position should be used as a conversation starter and to provide top cover for your team.

Rewarding your team is also a way to show your power and influence, but once again, this can be abused and misused. As a leader, you must understand how your people want to be rewarded. Some people have rooms filled with plaques and awards that they were presented for doing a good job, and that is important to them. Others may not want the public recognition but will be thrilled to be given a new project to work on. The point is that using rewards as a source of exuding power and influence can be done well if you understand what motivates your individual team members.

The final power and influence concept we covered revolved around expertise. Traci is an expert. She has the academic background and experience to talk circles around most people, but she doesn't. Traci uses her expertise to teach and to learn. When we reach what we think is the peak of our professional knowledge base, we can tend to overlook or even discount other ideas. We can use our power and influence to teach, protect our people, and drive decision making, or we can use it to bully, manipulate, and climb over people on our way to the top. But building a legacy isn't about bullying or manipulation.

We ended our leadership walk by discussing building a legacy. This is what it all comes down to. What do you leave behind once you log off for the last time? Have you led in a way that others will want to follow and emulate? This is the culmination of a leadership life lived well. What kinds of leaders have you developed? Would you want your kids to work for the organization you've built?

These are tough questions, but the answers are really the whole point of this book. The world of hybrid leadership has changed the way we think of legacy and leadership. Leadership, now more than ever, needs to be more personal. A lot of us don't have the ability to pop into a teammate's cubicle and check in on them. We must be intentional. Does this mean that we have to give in to every request or need that our people have? No. Do we need to walk on eggshells regarding requirements and business needs? No. What we need to do is understand the ecosystem of our teams by understanding each individual's skill set, mind-sets, and motivations and use them to drive the business and empower the people. Hybrid work has challenged this, but we are up for the challenge.

With so many advantages, remote and hybrid work is here to stay. No commute time, increased ability to get things done around the house, and the ability to work from anywhere. Yes, there are inherent leadership challenges surrounding accountability and productivity, but these can be countered by clear performance metrics and communication.

Thank you for trusting me through this. I know there are several other leadership books that you could have picked up, but I'm confident the tools I've presented will equip you with what you need to be successful. I'll say it again: hybrid leadership, by design, challenges many of the old-school leadership models that were so successful for on-site teams, but what it also does is provide us with new opportunities to get to know our people and how they operate. Take care of your people, take care of yourself, and create a community that will support you and push you to be a better leader. Start strong, and finish well!

FINAL TANGIBLE TRANSFORMATION TIPS FOR HYBRID WORK

1. Have a "camera on" policy for meetings. Unless they are in the car, their cameras should be on.

2. Have your one-on-ones in the office if possible. If it's not possible, remember, camera on.

3. If your team is local, or some members are local, have them come into the office at least one day a week and overlap them with another coworker. This will help with team cohesion.

4. Start virtual meetings ten minutes early and end them ten minutes late. This will give the team a chance to catch up and talk shop before the team begins with official business. It's not mandatory for them to show up early or stay late, but I'll bet they do anyway.

5. Be available but not on call. You have a job to do as well. Individual consideration doesn't mean that you are there to meet your team's every need whenever they need it. Create "office hours" where you will be available to talk about your team's concerns and needs.

6. Help your people get out of the house. Challenge your people. Have fun with it. Create physical or mental challenges that have nothing to do with the business.

NOTES

Introduction

1   Eleena De Lisser, "The Virtual Office," *Wall Street Journal*, March 19, 2001, https://www.wsj.com/articles/SB984591445363850574.

2   Luis L. Martins, Lucy L. Gilson, and M. Travis Maynard, "Virtual Teams: What Do We Know and Where Do We Go from Here?" *Journal of Management* 30, no. 6 (November 2004), 805–35, https://doi.org/10.1016/j.jm.2004.05.002, ScienceDirect. com, https://www.sciencedirect.com/science/article/abs/pii/ S0149206304000649.

3   Heather Long and Andrew Van Dam "U.S. unemployment rate soars to 14.7 percent, the worst since the Depression era" *Wall Street Journal*, March 8, 2020, https://www.washingtonpost.com/ business/2020/05/08/april-2020-jobs-report/

Chapter 1 – Transformational Leadership: Inspiring and Motivating Individuals

1   Jan Stewart, *Transformational Leadership: An Evolving Concept Examined through the Works of Burns, Bass, Avolio, and Leithwood,* 2017.

2   Fatmah Hussein Jaafari, "A Theoretical Understanding of Transformational Leadership," *International Journal of Development Research*, 2019, Volume 09. https://www.journalijdr.com/ theoretical-understanding-transformational-leadership

3   James MacGregor Burns, *Leadership* (New York: Harper & Row, 1978), pg 460 and 462.

4   Barbara Z. Larson, Susan R. Vroman, and Erin E. Makarius, A Guide to Managing Your (Newly) Remote Workers, Harvard Business Review (2020)

5   Frates, Martino, Pegg, *American Journal of Lifestyle Medicine* (2017), 11(6), 466–475.

6   Ed Catmull, *Creativity Inc.*, Random House Publishing (2014)

Chapter 2 – What Would Kotter Do: Unpacking the Eight Steps of Organizational Change

1   John P. Kotter, *Leading Change: Why Transformation Efforts Fail* (Boston, Harvard Business School Press, 1996).

2   John P. Kotter, *A Sense of Urgency* (Boston: Harvard Business Press, 2008), 3.

Chapter 3 – Contingency Leadership: What Happens When the Stuff Hits the Fan

1   "The Contingency Theory of Leadership Explained," Villanova University, September 9, 2021, https://www.villanovau.com/resources/leadership/contingency-theory-leadership/.

2   "The Contingency Theory of Leadership Explained."

3   Fred E. Fiedler, "Leadership Experience and Organizational Performance," *United States Army Research Institute for the Behavioral and Social Sciences*, August 1997, 1–2, https://apps.dtic.mil/sti/pdfs/ADA335798.pdf.

Chapter 4 – Understanding the Individual: Inside Our Decision-Making Process

1   Urie Bronfenbrenner, *The Ecology of Human Development: Experiments by Nature and Design* (Cambridge, MA: Harvard University Press, 1979), 415.

2   Donald R. Haurin, Toby L. Parcel, and R. Jean Haurin, "The Impact of Homeownership on Child Outcomes," Joint Center for Housing Studies, Harvard University, October 2001, https://www.jchs.harvard.edu/sites/default/files/liho01-14.pdf.

3   Urie Bronfenbrenner, *The Ecology of Human Development*, 208.

4   Urie Bronfenbrenner, *The Ecology of Human Development*, 235.

5   Urie Bronfenbrenner, *The Ecology of Human Development*, chapter 11.

Chapter 5 – Innovation Leadership: How to Change the World

1   Joseph A. Schumpeter, *The theory of economic development: an inquiry into profits, capital, credit, interest, and the business cycle,* Transaction Publishers (1983)

2   "When, Why, and How to Use the Agile-Waterfall Hybrid Model," Intland Software, June 2021, https://content.intland.com/blog/agile/when-why-how-to-use-the-hybrid-model.

3   "Waterfall Methodology," Adobe Experience Cloud, accessed June 10, 2022, https://www.workfront.com/project-management/methodologies/waterfall#:~:text=The%20Waterfall%20methodology%20follows%20a,%2C%20are%20usually%20self%2Dcontained.

Chapter 6 – Power and Influence Theory: Using Your Powers for Good

1   J. R. P. French Jr. and B. H. Raven, "The Bases of Social Power," in D. Cartwright, ed., *Studies in Social Power* (Ann Arbor, MI: Institute for Social Research, 1959), 150–67.

Chapter 7 – Leaving a Legacy: Your Footprints in the Cultural Sand

1   "Selma to Montgomery March," Stanford University: The Martin Luther King, Jr. Research and Education Institute, n.d., accessed June 10, 2022, https://kinginstitute.stanford.edu/encyclopedia/selma-montgomery-march.

2   John C. Maxwell, *The 21 Irrefutable Laws of Leadership: Follow Them and People Will Follow You* (New York City: Harper Collins, 2001), 10.

ABOUT THE AUTHOR

Dr. Travis Hearne is a nine-year veteran of the United States Marine Corps, former government civilian working for the Intelligence Community and the Department of the Air Force, is currently a cybersecurity specialist for Cisco Systems and the CEO and founder of Titanium Leadership.

As a Marine, he served as a senior intelligence analyst with the 1st Light Armored Reconnaissance Battalion out of Camp Pendleton, California, leading teams to Iraq in support of Operation Iraqi Freedom from 2008 to 2009 and in Afghanistan in support of Operation Enduring Freedom in 2010. From 2011 to 2016 he served as a senior intelligence analyst at United States Northern Command (USNORTHCOM), leading teams focusing on the analysis of advanced threats to the homeland from terrorist organizations, transnational criminal organizations, and other state actors.

After his honorable discharge from the Marine Corps in 2016, Travis continued his service as a USNORTHCOM civilian, first as an intelligence officer for the Defense Intelligence Agency (DIA) responsible for managing teams focusing on threats to North America from terrorist groups, then as the team lead of an interagency task force focusing on decreasing the flow of narcotics into and out of the United States, and finally as the Chief Interagency and Operations Officer for

USNORTHCOM, heading up teams focusing on analyzing cybersecurity threat information.

Travis's passion is for equipping leaders, soon-to-be leaders, and organizations with tools to better lead their people; it's what gets him up in the morning. As the founder and principal consultant for Titanium Leadership Consulting, Travis provides his consulting services to executives and executive teams of large and small organizations alike, helping them to lead well and drive growth and success regardless of whether they are on-site, remote, or hybrid working environments.

Travis and his wife, Traci (sound familiar?), live in Colorado Springs, Colorado, and have three boys (Braden, Michael, and Brice). Travis leads a number of military and civilian small groups focusing on leadership and mentoring and serves as a leader in the men's and military ministries at New Life Church in Colorado Springs.

Printed in the USA
CPSIA information can be obtained
at www.ICGtesting.com
JSHW021006151023
50072JS00004B/139